Startup: Be the successful entrepreneur you want to be.

The concise guide to starting a business and getting it right the first time.

Frank Burke MBA

Contents

Copyright	1
Limit of Liability/Disclaimer of Warranty:	2
Dedication and Acknowledgements	3
Stage 1 - Planning	4
Chapter 1 - Introduction	5
Chapter 2 - Know Yourself	9
What Mindset are you?	9
Are you equipped to start a business?	11
Why do you want to start up a business?	12
Do you have to set up a business?	13
How good is your health?	15
Can you handle failure?	15
How good is your support network?	16
What's your knowledge/education level?	17
Motivation.	19
Are you really excited starting your business?	20
Do you feel that you satisfy a need within you?	20
Can I have down days?	20
Can you deal with resentment?	21
Chapter 3 - Goal Setting	23
Goal Setting.	23
Goals are a manifestation of what you want to achieve.	24
Setting goals that matter!	25
Quality of life goals.	25
Financial goal setting.	27
Be careful, goals can be limiting.	28
Chapter 4 - Reality Check	29

What are your resources?	29
Personal financial audit.	30
Your local government help network - how good is it?	33
Your time - it's valuable!	34
Chapter 5 - Feasibility Study	**36**
What is a feasibility study?	36
Proof of concept?	39
Do I really need a business plan to succeed?	42
Chapter 6 - Sole proprietor or Incorporation?	**46**
Should I incorporate or be a sole proprietor?	46
Don't lose your shirt!	47
What corporation structure is best for me?	49
Should I Incorporate with co-founders?	51
Sweat equity vs. financial equity.	52
Stage 2 - Liftoff	54
Chapter 7 - Strategy	**55**
Start with the end in mind.	55
From the beginning - plan to make yourself redundant!	56
Create a company built on systems, not people.	58
Self-efficiency.	60
Don't waste your time -	60
Plan your day.	61
Do what's most important first.	62
Adopt useful technology early.	63
The peril of putting your business before family.	64
Outsourcing and startups.	65
Are any customers or clients vampires?	67
It's OK to make mistakes!	68

Take heed of the economic cycle.	69
Chapter 8 - Marketing and Sales Strategy	**71**
Marketing and Sales.	71
Your customer is king!	72
A confused mind says no!	75
Sell the benefits, not the features.	75
It's sales that matter!	77
You should market yourself.	78
You do not get a second chance to make a first impression!	79
Copy what works.	80
Build a sales and referral network.	81
When a sales structure works.	82
Red Lines that can't be crossed.	84
Chapter 9 - Finance Strategy	**86**
Are you still in the twilight zone?	86
Hit the street running!	87
Focus on the cash flow!	88
Matching cash flow.	89
Do not give credit.	89
Checks or card payments?	91
Pre-payment is best.	91
Debt management.	92
Banks - Don't bank with one only.	92
Taxes - when to pay.	94
Get an accountant.	95
Do not run before you can walk.	95
At the breakeven point.	96
Never, ever, buy business!	98

What is value creation?	100
Chapter 10 - Your Business is About People	**103**
People are not economic units of production!	103
Start small think big.	103
Look for talent.	105
Money and what else?	106
Management by expectation.	107
Don't let flexibility be seen as weakness.	108
When a clone is desirable.	109
It's the team that wins.	110
Chapter 11 - Leadership	**112**
Share your vision.	112
Lead by example.	113
Earn respect.	114
Leaders take risks!	114
To gain, you have to sacrifice.	115
Work smarter and harder!	116
Leaders are made.	117
Stage 3 - Consolidation	119
Chapter 12 - Your Business is Changing!	**120**
When does a startup cease to be a startup?	120
Do not ease off the pedal!	121
Change management.	121
Investment for growth.	124
The big decision!	125
The last word.	126

Copyright

Copyright © 2016 by Frank Burke.

All rights reserved.

No part of this publication may be reproduced, stored in a retrieval system, or transmitted in whole or in part, in any form or by any means, electronic, mechanical, photocopying, recording, sharing, or otherwise, without the prior written permission of the author.

Inquiries regarding permission for use of the material contained in this book should be addressed to:

Francis Burke MBA

frank@francisburke.com

Limit of Liability/Disclaimer of Warranty:

This disclaimer governs the use of this book. By using this book, you accept this disclaimer in full.

While the authors have used their best efforts in preparing this book, they make no representations or warranties with respect to the accuracy or completeness of the contents of this book and specifically disclaim any implied warranties of merchantability or fitness for a particular purpose. You should consult with a professional where appropriate.

The advice and strategies contained herein may not be suitable for your situation. Neither the publisher nor author shall be liable for any loss of profit or any other commercial damages, including but not limited to special, incidental, consequential, or other damages. No warranty may be created or extended by sales representatives or written sales materials.

Dedication and Acknowledgements

This book is dedicated to my wife, Marina, for her tremendous patience and support.

Stage 1 - Planning

"Reduce your plan to writing. The moment you complete this, you will have definitely given concrete form to the intangible desire."

Napoleon Hill

Chapter 1 - Introduction

First of all, let me say thank you for purchasing my book. Let me also say that in this book I have endeavored to share with you my experience in setting up numerous businesses, and working as a consultant to over 100 companies in the United Kingdom and in the U.S. in the venture capital field.

So, why should you listen to me? The reason is simple. I have personally established businesses for others and myself. To be honest, I learned the most from one of my major failures, and the lesson was extremely painful both financially and motivationally. One should never be afraid of making mistakes, what one should be afraid of is quitting. However, it's from the failures in life that we learn the most.

For over 25 years, I have not only set up my own businesses but also helped others start up businesses. In the process of helping other people establish companies, I discovered there are many qualities necessary for a successful startup that not all entrepreneurs adhere to. The successful startup businesses had several things in common, and those that were unsuccessful also had several things in common. Most of the successful businesses I dealt with were incorporated and planned well. Those that were unsuccessful failed to plan or did not plan effectively.

There's an old saying, "fail to plan, plan to fail." I can honestly say, that inadequate planning at the pre-startup stage represents the first step to management failure, as failing to plan effectively or plan at all, is in itself a critical management deficiency.

So, I have structured this book in a logical way to reflect what works in the real world and what doesn't. The book is divided into three stages, and you may have already guessed, I will be starting with *Planning* as Stage I.

In this stage, I examine the mindset that is necessary for success. There are many startup books, which will put the mindset and motivational aspect towards the end of the book, this to me, is insanity.
Before you undertake any journey, you need to know where you're going, and how you're going to get there. When starting a business, you need to be aware of how you feel about it, what you want to do, i.e., and the goals that you're setting yourself and then move forward.

Without the proper mindset and goals, you will not be equipped to deal with the hard issues, both financial and psychological, as you move forward. Also in Stage I, we will be looking at a reality check to work out what your resources are concerning cash, access to credit or capital, your help network, the available time you have to work on the business and the state of your health. We look at the structure of the business, sole proprietor or incorporation, whether you will start up alone or have co-founders, which may or may not be investors. These factors will give you an idea of what you have to work with. Next, even though you may have a great idea, you have to prove the market exists, and ensure your customers or clients are getting what they want, not what you want to give them, and confirm that they will pay you for it.

It's in the planning stage that you can to set up a solid foundation.

Stage 2 starts the practical side of putting all the ideas into reality. At this stage, you need to focus more on the customer, especially on how you are going to create sustainable value for both the customer and your business. You should already have created a customer avatar in your planning stage (more on that later), but at this stage, you need to flesh things out. Here you also need to look at cash flow strategies and remember that in a startup, cash is king, if you run out of cash then you're no longer liquid, and quite literally your business will seize up!

Finally in this Stage, and I've seen it so many times, startups race ahead of themselves, and more often than not, some growth strategies are adopted that will eventually kill the business. We go into some of the pitfalls and their control measures that will provide reinforcement to the business going forward.

You see, the point here is that you don't want your business to remain a startup forever - do you? As soon as you have got past the liftoff stage your business has to grow, expand and mature. It can only do this if the original foundation, upon which it has been launched, is robust and scalable.

Stage 3 is short and sweet, and is all about the transition from startup to a successful business; building on the foundation set in the planning and liftoff stages.

At this stage you have to decide whether you are a startup entrepreneur, and sell to take on the next project, or you transform yourself into the owner of a going concern, and we will go over some of the important differences to consider here.

So let's get started!

Chapter 2 - Know Yourself

What Mindset are you?

Mindset - what is that? I've never heard this before when talking about starting up a business; I can hear you say. Well, just bear with me for a minute, and I will explain in the next few sentences how important it is to your success or failure!

Our mindset is the critical driving force for what we do and why we do it. Our mindset influences our motivation. Therefore, if you have the wrong mindset, then you will potentially suffer from poor motivation.

Without going overboard academically, it is sufficient to identify two types of mindset, the fixed mindset, and the growth mindset. The fixed mindset is more concerned with external influences such as wealth and image. The forces that drive motivation are external to you and, therefore, less under your control. For this reason, it is considered the weaker mindset to start a business. Research at Harvard and West Point Military Academy has shown that *internalized motivation* is much stronger than *externalized motivation*.

The growth mindset person recognizes abilities as changeable, and that these abilities or skills can be modified to suit changes in circumstances, and is more internalized - therefore, more controllable by the individual.

The entrepreneur typically has a growth mindset and the starting of a business is seen from the perspective of a journey rather than a distinct outcome. So, if you define yourself as having a growth mindset, your temperament and character may be more suited for starting up a business.

But what if you feel you have more of a fixed mindset than a growth mindset? Honestly, it's not a disaster, far from it. It means you have a different way of looking at things and, therefore, need to be aware of it to ensure you stay on the right track and get support where you need it. You can also recognize when you are thinking in a fixed manner and make the choice to think in a different way if you feel it will help.

If you are concerned, there is a lot of information available online that will help you. Also to add reassurance, there are some extremely successful entrepreneurs and businessmen like Donald Trump, who would fit potentially into the category of fixed mindset, and he's been very successful.

Success depends on so many factors, and every person

is individual, but the value of recognizing which mindset you fit into can be an invaluable place to start to ensure that you strengthen your motivational stamina for the journey ahead.

So, now you have figured out what mindset category you fit into, and are raring to go - steady on, there are a few more questions that need to be answered before you start your business, and these should be addressed first to improve your chances of success. Let's get going!

Are you equipped to start a business?

Ok, I can see you scratching your head and saying to yourself - What's this guy on about? I'm fired up and ready to go after the World, and he's suggesting that I may not be prepared sufficiently to get the ball rolling! This guy is a motivation killer! In fact, the opposite is true.

An athlete before running a race prepares mentally for it. How often have you read about sports people playing the shot in their mind before taking the shot at the basket, or the runner who visualizes how he or she is going to run the race; this is mental preparation. The athlete that wins is often the one that has done the most physical and mental preparation by working behind the scenes, training. Moreover, the training is utilized to perfect existing strengths, and lessen the effects of weaknesses when it comes to beating the competition.

The athletes, therefore, must equip themselves with those necessary attributes that will win the race or the game. Starting a business is similar to being an athlete - you have to get out there and fight to win. You have to be better than the competition. You have to do things better than the competition - you have to be the competitor to beat!

Successful people, whether in business or sport, are experts at self-examination. It is through this process that they know where to target their resources. It is no coincidence that most people learn more from their failures than from their successes. It is at the point of failure that a person gets to know himself or herself better, their strengths and their weaknesses and can, therefore, work on them to achieve their goals in life.

Now I hear you asking how do I know if I am prepared to start this adventure? Well, there are a few fundamental questions. Don't be fooled by their simplicity. Simple questions are often the hardest to answer truthfully!

Why do you want to start up a business?

There is no right or wrong answer here - you just have to be very clear to yourself to answer the *Why*. Is it that you have been made unemployed, and you can't find a job? Is it because you want more challenge because life working for someone is boring? Is it because you have just come out of College, and you don't wish to work in a nine to five job? There is a reason for wanting to set up a business - find it!

If the reason to start lacks enthusiasm, determination and a willingness to self-sacrifice then think again about your decision as this may not be the right course of action for you.

Do you have to set up a business?

Asking this is crucial, so take care in answering it. If you have to start a business, this can have two important connotations. The first meaning attributable can point to desperation on your part, possibly as a response to not being able to find the right job and, therefore, the thought that it's better to do something, than nothing prevails. While desperation can be a fantastic motivator, most times it is not, as research has shown that 'desperation' as a motivator is more of an escape clause for getting out of certain adverse situations in your personal life.

Many people in this situation find themselves clutching at straws in a reactionary sense, and this is bad news. Having said that, I have come across success stories, and

I'm sure so have you, but remember people don't broadcast their failures, so successes are usually the tip of the iceberg.

If you find that you are in a financially dangerous situation, you will still need to plan, and will have to look at businesses that do not require a cash outlay, but can generate quick cash. These startups can succeed, but remember; in life you must pay with something - either cash or in time and sweat equity.

Now, the other side of *have to* is idea driven and backed by abundant energy and enthusiasm. A fact of life is that those people that are motivated by ideals or ideas are those most likely to succeed. However, what I have seen in my experience is that those qualities plus a dose of good old fortitude make an even better combination. All too often I have seen idealistic, and enthusiastic *wannabe* entrepreneurs give up at the first hurdle!

Starting a business is a very stressful period in your life. Yes, it can be exciting but nonetheless, stressful. It is both mentally and physically demanding and exhausting, and you have to keep going. It is here when three factors come into play, your positive mindset, and mental and physical stamina; this leads to an often-overlooked question, which you must ask.

How good is your health?

How often have you heard the expression that the mind is willing, but the body is weak. Whether we like it or not, the body wears out and the stresses of modern day life take their toll.

We are getting older; things in our body and our mind don't work as well; we wear out. So it's a good idea to know your general level of health. The reason is that, for example, if you're over 50, and you find out that your heart is not as healthy as it could be, then you have to find a way of reducing the stress.

You have to ensure that you have the necessary physical and mental stamina to get through hard times and push the business forward in the good times.

Can you handle failure?

Don't be fooled by the management gurus that tell you failure is not an option. It is an option, but it doesn't have to be damaging if you can make good use of the lessons learned by failing. In fact, some of the top CEO's of companies will not hire people who state that they have never failed; those that say this are either lying or crazy or even both! I love the inspirational quote from one of my heroes Winston Churchill when he said,

"Success consists of going from failure to failure without loss of enthusiasm."

You should aim for success in everything you do, but if you can't handle failure either in yourself or others you will have to find a mechanism to deal with it - trust me, your success will depend on it.

How good is your support network?

There are two types of support network personal and professional. You will need both!

No person is an island. There are times when we need someone we can trust; however when it comes to business you have to be careful. I don't mean this to offend anyone but families, and close friends are often the greatest de-motivators. I'm not malicious, here; more often than not it's the opposite situation - a genuine concern where they don't want to see you hurt. They don't want to see you lose money, and more so, they don't want to see you suffer mentally the pain of failure. They would prefer you to get a safe and secure job.

The prevailing attitude today is that we live in a cotton wool culture, so hurt is something that has to be avoided.

On the flip side of the coin, you can have family and

friends, who again don't want to hurt your feelings and ego, and will support you as you literally go over a cliff. Neither is desirable. So, of extreme importance is to seek out a professional support network.

It is a good idea to join your local chamber of commerce. It is here that you will get concrete advice from entrepreneurs and business people who are either developing their business or those who are like-minded and have started their own. The members know what you're going through - they've been there and done that, and are often a wealth of information.

Many times I have talked to retired members of various chambers, and they are bored with retirement, and are genuinely looking to help a fellow entrepreneurial soul!

Don't overlook this valuable resource. Importantly, relationships here will help counter, if needs be, the not so objective concerns that your personal network may show.

What's your knowledge/education level?

You need to ask this question, and it might sound like a strange question, but it's necessary to answer. Do not confuse knowledge with education. Some of the richest men and women in the world do not have a qualification higher than a high school diploma, but their knowledge about markets, human relationships in business, the products, and services that they deliver to customers and clients, is second to none.

These people are often the *doers*, they get on with things; they recognize that they are not academics - so what do they do? They hire smarter people than them to do the things they can't do. That is not to say that education is useless in a business environment. Quite the contrary, it's very useful but it's not essential, and that is the main thing to consider.

It is, however, necessary to increase your knowledge by educating yourself on important things that concern your business. Information learned about the Economy and Finance, in particular, will come in useful, especially when you need to develop strategies to move the company forward past the startup phase. Remember knowledge is power only when it is used.

So do not underestimate the importance that a good mindset is to the success of your startup. It's essential that you know yourself, your capabilities and limits, so as you can plan to move forward, and knowing what is more likely to work for you starting a business.

The ancient Greek Philosopher, Socrates stated that,

"to know yourself is the greatest road to wisdom"

You need to be wise and objective so as you make the best decisions, and which advice, in particular, is best to take and act upon when needed.

Ok, now we have looked at the importance of mindset; let's now see the importance of staying motivated.

Motivation.

Motivation is the reason or reasons we have for acting or behaving in a particular way, and is either intrinsic (internally driven) or extrinsic (externally driven). As mentioned before in the opening section on mindset; our intensity of motivation and its durability is dependent to a significant extent on our prevailing mindset. So it's important to drill down with a few questions and see how durable or fragile our level of motivation is before starting the business.

I would assume as the reader of this book your motivational levels are quite high, and you are keen to get into more detail about actually setting up the business. Great, but bear with me with just a little more patience!

Are you really excited at the prospect of starting your business?

If you're excited, it's a great sign. You have a positive attitude. When you love what you do, it never feels like work. If it feels like work, then get a job.

When I was setting up some of my businesses, the thrill of starting something new compensated for the long hours, but it never never felt like work. When talking to many of the people I have helped their experience has been the same.

Do you feel that you satisfy a need within you?

When Monday morning comes you should feel a sense of enthusiasm, a challenge, an opportunity to excel, and you should feel like you are creating something, a part of yourself.

For me, for example, starting a business from scratch, developing and then selling it gives me a tremendous sense of satisfaction and achievement - it's a great buzz to create something out of an idea and create value! Your need may be different, but nearly all entrepreneurs start a business to satisfy a deep need, and that is what sustains the motivation.

Can I have down days?

Of course, you can, is the short answer. In fact, if you

didn't have those days when nothing seems to work out and it saps your enthusiasm you wouldn't be human. You have to recognize within yourself that what you're feeling is natural and normal in a startup environment. When you feel like this, is when it's an opportunity to tap into your professional network organization that you are a member of, and get out and meet some people with enthusiasm, and have a coffee and don't feel guilty about it. By networking positively you are contributing to your business. You are dealing with a down day by making it positive and at the same time just possibly taking a well-earned break.

Can you deal with resentment?

When running a business you often have to fire people that are close to you, even friends and yes on occasions even business partners. In a startup business, you are on a learning curve and quite often employees you hire and even people you work with do not possess the necessary abilities to carry out essential tasks. As a result, you have to let go of or fire unproductive people. It's sad, but it is a fact of business life. What seems like a cold and brutal act, often is, and can cause resentment from people close to you and sap your motivation.

It can drain your enthusiasm quickly if you don't have a mechanism set in place to deal with it. Ultimately you have to toughen up, and the best mechanism to deal with it is to ignore resentment, but at the same time don't chase respect as compensation - earn respect. Respect earned from employees and peers is a great source of motivation moving forward.

Chapter 3 - Goal Setting

Goal Setting.

A goal is the object of a person's ambition or effort and is also an aim or desired result. A business comprises a combination of goals that are developed initially at startup and gradually over time as the business changes. These are measurable and often time specific and can be changeable. In a nutshell, though, the primary goal of a business is to grow profitably. Without growth, a business will deteriorate to nothing and without profit, a business will cease to exist eventually. Every other goal, whether, intentional or not is *bolted on* to these two central imperatives.

Be under no illusion, the initial goals of the entrepreneur in starting up a business will influence the strategies adopted later. You will often read or hear people talking about marketing strategy and operational strategy etc., these are the tactics adopted to realize these goals. So the bottom line here is if you get your initial goals wrong no matter what strategies you adopt, there's a high probability the business will fail. Get the goals right at the start with good strategies and you have a much better platform for success.

Goals are a manifestation of what you want to achieve.

As an entrepreneur, it is important to recognize that goals do not materialize out of thin air nor should they be kept your personal property. It is often hard for individuals to express internalized goals because they feel them and that is why it's important to write them down and clarify them. If you can't understand your goals when you write them down how do you expect others in the company to understand them as well?

The writing down of your goals is important because this represents visible milestones upon which you will be able to measure your progress and so are crucial markers in your journey.

Research has also shown that the visualization of goals is also a vital source of motivation and provides a much-needed compass when the going gets tough.

I have never come across a successful startup or company that did not have clear, achievable goals that were communicated throughout the business.

In setting goals, you should prioritize your goals, in particular, the ones that materially affect the business. Those entrepreneurs, who are reading this book, if you haven't written down and classified your goals, do it now!

Setting goals that matter!

Previously I mentioned about prioritizing goals. These are the goals that are important to the business. However you are a person, not a machine, and for this reason, you need to divide your goals into two main areas - personal and business. Often there is overlap, fine, but still sort them into their relevant category.

Personal goals often relate to the quality of life that the entrepreneur wants to achieve, and the business is a means to achieve those goals. On the other hand, the entrepreneurs' goal can also be to create a business to satisfy financial goals first, and then *indirectly* satisfy goals related to the quality of life desired. Very rarely is a business created for the sake of starting a business; there is usually a fundamental reason or reasons for doing it. Whichever one of these paths you take is fine as long as you identify why you are taking that path.

Now, let's look at some of these goals.

Quality of life goals.

Most executive management jobs are not nine to five, it's more common, especially in London to be working 8 am to 7 pm and even weekends when major projects are due. In fact, the higher your pay grade, the more the company expects of you, and moreover, it's not uncommon to feel *owned* - literally a part of the assets of the company. Many of the entrepreneurs I helped start their companies wanted to spend more time with their family and have more control over their lives. The money was not the primary objective, although extremely important.

Other entrepreneur's set up businesses to take advantage of hobbies that can be monetized, for example, I have a good friend who loves travel and runs a travel blog and has sponsors. He can travel the world and make money at the same time!

Other quality of life goals can literally be a desired way of life. Another one of my friends traded in a high pressure (very highly paid) banking position to breed alpacas. It's now a thriving family business and very profitable.

The important thing to remember about a business is that it should always be viewed as a business that must turn a profit otherwise the desired quality of life will not materialize. A balance must be struck.

Now on to financial goals which many of you will be more familiar with.

Financial goal setting.

Financial goals can be both personal and business, and are often the easiest to set and the hardest to achieve. One of the main reasons for this is that personal goals, in the main, are usually more internalized and less influenced by external factors.

Financial goals are more exposed to external factors, both personal and business. For example, during the Great Crisis of 2008, corporate liquidity dried up when banks stopped lending to each other, putting many companies out of business that would have otherwise survived, subsequently causing many individuals to file unexpectedly for bankruptcy.

Like all goals, financial goals, in particular, can be quite specific when related to the direct functioning of the business because they have to be, for example, the setting of financial targets and debt limits. However financial goals often overlap into the personal goal realm, for example, the entrepreneur may formulate a financial goal where income from the company is to fund his 401k for retirement. A short-term goal may be for the person to use profits to get out of personal debt, and another to become financially independent.

Setting goals should not be a once and done affair.

Goals should be revisited to ensure that they are being achieved and amended where necessary; this is especially true where the goals are specific and target related, i.e., getting out of debt. Obviously, when you have achieved that, you can score this item off your list, and perhaps add a goal of having $15,000 in your personal savings account at the end of the financial year.

Goal formation should be fluid. However, your core personal and business goals should remain steady. Otherwise, you will enter a state of strategic and motivational drift.

Be careful, goals can be limiting.

If you are a creative entrepreneur, goals can be very limiting. Imagine having set goals on Steve Jobs, or Thomas Edison, we would never have iPhones, iTunes, and the light bulb. Goals are there to provide a focus for your entrepreneurial energy. They should not be there to extinguish the very heart of your business if it relies on creativity; there must be a balance struck. Very rarely do we come across in business an inventor and a great businessperson like James Dyson. Many successful businesses have more than one founder where one is the *creative genius* and the other is the *business brain* that puts the structure together and commercializes the idea.

Chapter 4 - Reality Check

What are your resources?

I cover this as you need to measure your net resources and where your resources are deficient, the steps required to rectify the situation. The reason I say this is because the amount of resources you have will dictate how you start. For example, if you have no cash, access to credit and no family with sufficient funds to lend to you, then the way you start your business is going to be entirely different to someone who has cash, and credit.

Think of it like this, would you go into battle without guns and ammunition? No, it would be suicide. Now, I am not saying don't attempt to start a business because you have no capital. Quite the contrary. It just means that you have to build up the resources to finance the business and pay your bills - it's just another step that you have to add. In fact, starting from nothing with your back up against the wall is an incredibly strong motivational factor, and many successful businesses have started that way. For example, Steve Jobs started in a garage with a few friends, Mike Dell had a similar start. The important thing is they used what resources they had and went for that *break* that would propel the business forward.

In my experience businesses that have started resource-rich often floundered because the entrepreneur either did not have or lost that sense of urgency or hunger often necessary to kick start the business.

Personal financial audit.

To do this, you sit down with a pen and paper or your laptop and prepare seven sheets on a spreadsheet. In sheet one, you would put your sources of income from your regular day job (if you have one), from investments and anything that contributes to your monthly income. In sheet two you would put your expenses including rent or mortgage, utility bills, loans and every outgoing expense you have in the month. Be thorough and honest with the information in these two columns. Subtracting the figure on sheet two from the figure on sheet one will give your net cash inflow or outflow.

In sheet three you need to list the value all your assets. In this column, you should put the value of your house, even though this is technically not an asset if it still has a mortgage on it, and your car even though you may have a car loan on it. I will explain later why you need to do this. In sheet four list all your outstanding debts, this would include the amount left on your mortgage if you have one, and the outstanding amount of your car loan, etc. Subtracting the amount on sheet four from the amount on sheet three will give your *net assets* or *net liabilities*.

In sheet five you need to put in the amount of credit you have access to at present; this would include the balance left on your credit cards.

In sheet six you would put the amount of capital you could access externally, for example, loans you would get from family members and or friends and your bank; if you have retirement investments that you are prepared to risk then put them in this column as well.

In sheet seven you would have a summary listing the figures from the previous sheets.

Now, you can look at sheet seven. The difference between cash in and your cash out, the first two columns; if it's negative, look and see what you can cut back on to make it balance or be cash flow positive. The more cash neutral to cash positive you are the better.

In subtracting the result of sheet four from three, you will be able to see what value your net assets are. If this is positive, then you may have to pledge your net assets as a guarantee for a bank loan. It is unlikely that a bank or financial institution is going to lend you money if you are cash flow negative and have negative net asset worth.

In sheet five, if for example, you have available credit on your credit cards, keep it in reserve. Some entrepreneurs have financed their startups by credit card when they were cash or asset poor, but it is an extremely expensive way of financing your startup and can cause you personal cash flow problems later trying to service the debt. It is last resort financing!

If you find that you are cash flow negative, have no credit and have zero to negative net asset value, then a source of funding can be family or friends; this can be organized as a backup. Be prepared for family problems if you can't pay back a loan; so make sure that if you borrow they understand that their capital is at risk. In this situation, you will most likely need to give equity for capital. Nothing in this life is free!

For retirement savings, these should be sacrosanct. If you're in the position that you have to dip into these savings, I would say that the writing is on the wall. You have to set some limits. I know that there are some amongst you who would be saying that business is all or nothing - well let me tell you that from personal experience *nothing* is very unpleasant!

Now at a glance, you can see in one place the extent of your financial health, your liabilities, your strengths and areas that you can work on to improve your financial foundation before starting. For example, in sheet six if you're unsure about how much your bank will advance you try to get a pre-agreed loan where you don't pay until you have a drawdown. Get some firm commitments from friends or family for amounts but remember you will in most cases have to trade equity for capital.

Your local government help network - how good is it?

We touched on having a good help network in the last chapter that was important for maintaining motivation, meeting like-minded people, and seeking objective advice and support.

There is another aspect to help networks that should be mentioned here that can provide financial savings. In the U.K., Europe and the U.S.A., there are business incubator services that are run by local government organizations. They offer very reasonably priced office accommodation and facilities, meeting rooms and secretarial services at a fraction of the cost of Main Street. You would be surprised to learn how many grants are available for certain types of startups, and as I said before, local chambers can often help by matching you up with a mentor.

Anything that adds value to your business at the startup stage while keeping your costs low is worth finding out!

Your time - it's valuable!

How often have you heard the maxim "time is money"? Well in business that could never be truer. Let's face it when you go to your auto mechanic you're charged $100 per hour, not a fixed price - if their time is money and you're willing to pay for it, then you should also cost out your time!

Many entrepreneurs fail to allocate time appropriately. You have 168 hours per week of which 45 to 60 is spent sleeping. That leaves 110 to 120 hours for other activities, and I'm sure you could not work those hours without killing yourself very quickly. Remember a *tired mind makes bad decisions*. So, if you're still in a paid job, after office hours, the commute and meal times, you are lucky if you have 20 hours to spend on your business. How are you going to spend that time? You need to have a priority system in place. Otherwise, you will never get done what is necessary. If you don't have a job then to a certain extent, you're not making any money, so the time you put in has to have a return. Otherwise, your personal finances are going to be in a very serious situation if you don't have sufficient resources on hand to cover your outlays.

A reality check is really a snapshot of what you have available to invest in your startup or the funding you will need to find when you do a more in-depth financial plan later.

At least after completing this stage you will have a better idea of what your resources are, and importantly you will have at hand a route to accessing the extra capital needed.

Chapter 5 - Feasibility Study

What is a feasibility study?

"Hold your horses - You have a great idea let's do the research."

A feasibility study is simply an analysis on the practicality of a proposed business and is done to ascertain whether the proposal is technically feasible, doable within the proposed cost structure and whether it will be profitable.

You have to prove a market exists for your business idea; you have to talk to potential customers and get a feel for what they want and don't want. Many times entrepreneurs are great at selling the idea, but when it comes to the sale, the customers and or clients do not wish to part with their money. This time is ideal to fine tune or amend the proposal.

There are some circumstances, however, especially in a services related business where you can test the viability by going to the market directly; this is what I call a hands-on practical feasibility study. For example, I had the pleasure of helping three college graduates set up a software services company where the concept was to provide small businesses with help in installing and running a content management system that could be customized. Their initial idea was to sell the installation and then get referrals.

When I met them, they were buzzing with energy, which was great, and then I asked them had they made any sales yet. The answer was no, but they *knew* it was a very good idea. To be honest, my gut feeling was also that it was an excellent idea, but I wanted them to prove to both themselves and me that there was a market there! I wanted them to test the market and prove that the business was feasible. The three of them made a good team as they had complementary skills, one was very good at selling, the other two were more nerdy, but very competent.

To the guy who was the better sales person, I suggested over the next week to go and get some sales and we would meet the Tuesday after that, and we would discuss the sales figures and get feedback. When we had the meeting, he had seven sales, which he made over four days. His other two partners installed the software over three days for their new clients. As you can image the three of them were excited, WOW, they made sales and profit. The problem was, as I had seen it, that there were seven sales and three people to be paid, plus expenses and it wouldn't take much time before they were at full capacity with limited income potential.

We had a talk, and I asked one of them, (not the sales guy) if there had been any follow-up phone calls after the installation. No, was the answer. So I suggested that he phone one of the new clients and ask what extra work they could do; the reply was quite surprising. The client needed the content management system, but they needed someone to keep it up to date, and potentially modify aspects of it to suit their business. The company then asked would they be willing to maintain the system for them; the answer from the team was yes!

After the phone call, I suggested a residual cash flow model, i.e., charge monthly. After the first month the business revenue was $4,000 and after twelve months monthly residual income from clients was $125,000, that's $1,500,000 annual turnover. Net profit was extremely high as they were not chasing their tails for new business, which allowed them to work on their business, not in it!

It was after the business idea was validated, that a detailed business plan was set up.

The point I'm making here is that this business idea was validated by proving that sales could be made and that there was a sustainable revenue and profit stream there; this was a practical feasibility study and proof of concept rolled into one.

Following this strategy is riskier, and adheres more to the idea that it is better to succeed fast or fail fast, and is a popular example of how startups can be accomplished with little cash.

Proof of concept?

Proof of concept is where you stretch the boundaries of the feasibility study to its breaking point, or points. It's proving that the business idea works by playing a devil's advocate role. You're looking for that stumbling block that you can't get over that kills the idea. It's where you look for the killer that will derail your business. It's the point where you have identified an insurmountable barrier that you cannot overcome, and that is not insuperable by hiring external help. Get past this and you have a business that has a high probability of success.

How do you prove the business? Do a test run, yes a test run. If it's a product or service, try and sell it. I can hear you ask - but I haven't got my product or service available? Then sell the idea, get some commitments.

Think of it like this, many realtors sell their houses or apartments off-plan!

Now you have some idea as to how hard, easy or difficult it is to sell. For example, the insurmountable barrier that you may experience is that a competitor has an identical product or service that is much cheaper and have better quality. In other words, you haven't done your marketing competitor analysis thoroughly. The question then becomes can you compete? Yes or No. If no, go back to the drawing board.

This process helps to isolate any weak parts in the feasibility study. It's the weak parts and the hurdles at the beginning of startups that are ticking time bombs if not identified. Most entrepreneurs are very good at identifying the strengths of their ideas but tend to overlook the weaknesses.

I have found that most entrepreneurs see much more clearly the strengths and opportunities of their idea, but gloss over the threats and weaknesses. More often than not, in those businesses that fail, the weaknesses have been in plain sight!

The amount of times I've heard entrepreneurs state that their idea is fabulous and that there is no doubt that the business is going to work, and they'll be rich is unbelievable. Hey, I'm not mocking enthusiasm, it often makes the difference between success and failure, BUT just because you think you have proven something to yourself doesn't mean that the market accepts your opinion, because that's just what it is.

The reasoning is quite simple. Until your product and service are sellable repeatedly, and at a profit you haven't got a business - it's still just an idea, it's still just your opinion!

People are naturally optimistic, especially entrepreneurs. If an entrepreneur is not optimistic and enthusiastic about the product or service, then the business is finished before it's even started. However, all the enthusiasm in the world is not going to resurrect a business that has no willing customers to part with money in a value exchange.

Ultimately, customers part with money to purchase something that is of greater value to them now than holding the cash. There must be a need or desire for that customer to buy from you and become a client now! I put in this immediacy element because you are starting a business now. You do not have a going concern where the company has three months of back orders and or clients coming in via the referral funnel. You haven't got off the ground running yet! You haven't proven that you have a viable business.

You need to prove the business idea. Some entrepreneurs prefer to prepare an in-depth feasibility study on paper, and then get boots on the ground and get sales. This method is usually the preferred way of doing things if you're after finance or if it makes you more comfortable, and is necessary going forward.

Never, never go into business without a feasibility study and a plan. Period!

Do I really need a business plan to succeed?

The short answer is no, but there is an extremely high probability that your business will fail without one. You might get past the startup stage but after that at some point, you will hit a brick wall. Look at it this way, before GPS we used maps to get to our destination. A map, simply put, is a pictorial representation of a route we can take on a journey to a destination. The business plan is the route that we will take to get to our destination of a successful business! Without it, there is a high probability we will get lost.

There is no point in doing a business plan until you have done a feasibility study and a proof of concept. Many times you will hear advice to prepare a detailed business plan before you start a business. It sounds good on paper, but more often than not, in the real world of startups, this is a waste of energy because there are so many unknown factors that you discover that you haven't covered, and you need to start again.

What you have to prepare is a comprehensive plan that addresses all the issues that the business needs to succeed now, nothing more and nothing less. The plan truly becomes academic if there is no reality to substantiate it, and has to be foundational, something that you can build upon.

When preparing your plan - you have to ask yourself who's this plan for, investors or me? If it's me, then twenty pages should be sufficient, you don't even have to worry about formatting, and it's presentability! However, if it's for investors, then the formatting and content must also sell the business investment in a realistic way.

I have seen business plans up to eighty pages for small startups with incredible detail that was unnecessary and could have been edited to ten or fifteen pages with most of the information being superfluous. On the other hand, I have also seen plans of three to five pages that were lacking in any detail whatsoever. When working in the venture capital investment field, it was rare to see a plan of fewer than twenty pages or more than forty with an additional one to three-page summary.

For investors, your business plan needs to address a problem or genuine pain by presenting a solution to that dilemma that the customer faces. They want to see that you focus your strategy where there is a large market with potential for sales, and with a proven distribution channel strategy and even better, proof that the market is there via sales already generated; hence the importance of the proof of concept stage.

Just because you may have a unique angle or product does not mean that you have no competition. The moment you fail to identify competition (unless you have something never invented before), you will have blown yourself out of the water. Every business has competition! If there has been no competition identified, then the investor could rightly think that there is no market there!

Your startup business plan should reflect the stage you are now. Its purpose is to get your enterprise off the ground. It should encompass the core idea(s) of the business, who your customers are, and how you are going to acquire sales and or clients. It should include your financial budget, i.e., a spreadsheet of revenue and costs, with special attention to *cash burn* (the amount of money spent before breaking even), and breakeven analysis, and the structure of the business, i.e., Sole Proprietorship or Incorporation.

You also need to identify risks, such as technical, operational, market, management and legal. By spelling out the risks to the investor, this will demonstrate that you consider risk mitigation important. Your business plan, while providing a model for action, should be flexible to reflect a change in circumstances as opportunities arise.

My advice to entrepreneurs is after the feasibility study, and proof of concept has been done, is to construct a business plan that you would present to an investor. Imagine yourself as an investor - would he invest in your enterprise? What questions would he ask? Are they the questions you have asked yourself? You need to be thoroughly honest here; this becomes your blueprint for action.

Chapter 6 - Sole proprietor or Incorporation?

Should I incorporate or be a sole proprietor?

I can hear the questions from you - Why are you considering this now? Why didn't you raise this earlier in your planning section?

Let us draw an analogy here to explain why. When you go to a restaurant, the only criteria for you being there are the quality of the food and if you're on a budget, the quality for the price. You are not so worried about the structure of the management of the restaurant. In fact, if you were to visit the kitchen you probably wouldn't eat there!

The point is that your end customer is buying a product or service. They're not too worried about your business structure. If it's a product, then they are most likely going to be worried about two things. Firstly the guarantee, and secondly, if you're going to be around to service that product. If it's a service business then the two things that are going to concern them are your availability and your competence. If the business is small and personalized then being a sole proprietor is fine, however as you grow it's not.

The larger you grow, even as a startup, the more complicated running the business becomes. There are personal tax issues, for example, that get mixed in with the business taxes, and you will still need professional help, such as a good attorney and an accountant. In my experience, it has always been better to incorporate before hitting the ground with sales.

Don't lose your shirt!

Incorporation has many advantages over operating as a sole proprietor. Firstly businesses fail and succeed, but sadly most fail. Having a good lawyer incorporate your business will shield your personal assets, to some extent, from financial failure of the company. Secondly, having done the feasibility study and proof of concept, you may find that one funding option open to you is bank financing. It's a fact of life that finance is difficult to get for startups, but it is even harder for non-incorporated startups that have growth ambitions.

You should plan to incorporate when the company is in the proof of concept stage, and after the feasibility study comes out positively for the business, not before.

Business angel investors and venture capitalists often create a new incorporation for investments they make because there is a new structure of ownership within the company. From my experience, where, as an investor, a great new business has come up, often a new business plan is drawn up, and the business is then incorporated, not the other way around.

When to incorporate for an individual is a matter of choice. Many of the clients I have consulted have opted to incorporate while doing the feasibility study as it gave them a focus, having a business to build!

There's a smart way to do business, and then there is the naive way! I have just mentioned that there are certain benefits to incorporating; one of the main ones is limiting your liability, should your enterprise fail.

The bottom line is that incorporating, shields your personal assets in a way that being a sole proprietor cannot.

As a sole proprietor; You, the owner, assumes personal liability for losses made and financial obligations that you enter into. Your personal assets, such as your home, your car and anything you possess are at risk.

The only advantage to this structure is that it is easy, cheap and simple to maintain. However, if you are looking at setting up a larger business with employees, this structure puts your assets at risk. You have to ask yourself the question, knowing that there is a high failure rate with startups; is this the type of risk exposure you are happy with?

A corporation, on the other hand, is a separate legal entity from its owners. The crucial difference from the sole proprietorship model is that the corporation is the entity where the liabilities lie. For example, an individual, or company, which transacts business with your company, can claim against the assets of the company, not individuals within it.

A good example of this structure in operation is a listed company on the Dow Jones or S & P 500. If any of the companies on these indexes goes broke, the shareholders lose the value of their shares, not their personal assets.

This protection, however, can be limited, where the directors provide personal guarantees for mortgages and overdraft facilities from banks.

What corporation structure is best for me?

Most incorporations in the U.S. are C-Corporations. Besides having the benefits of liability separation, there is the ability to claim allowable business expenses against profits. Another major benefit over a sole proprietorship is continuity; the corporation will survive the owner's death.

These companies are more expensive than the sole proprietorship to set up and maintain. Annual accounts have to be filed, and there is more administration work required. The C- Corporation, has a tax disadvantage where income may be taxed twice, once at the corporate level, and again when distributed as dividend income to its owners.

The S-Corporation, however, offers many of the advantages of a C-Corporation, and has one major advantage, and that is the S-Corporation is taxed like the sole proprietorship and avoids the double taxation treatment of the C-Corporation. The status of a C-corporation can be changed to an S-Corporation by submitting a Form to the IRS (Form 2553).

The downside is that it is more expensive to set up and does not have all the tax-deductible benefits of a C-Corporation. There are two other limitations, in that, the shareholders must be U.S. Citizens, and it cannot be owned by another business; these are important to consider if you decide to sell the business after startup.

The other main corporate vehicle to shelter your liabilities is the Limited Liability Company, (LLC). This structure is a hybrid between the sole proprietorship and a corporation. It has all the legal separation protection of a corporation, but the taxation treatment is similar to the sole proprietorship.

Other advantages include easy management and pass-through taxation, (the owners pay taxes on all business profits on their individual tax returns).

A major potential disadvantage, though, is that there is no stock, and this can cause complications if the business expands and new stockholders want equity in your company.

However, whichever business structure you chose, the decision is not irreversible and can be changed. It's just an added expense later if you have to do so.

I strongly suggest, from personal experience, that you incorporate. Again, as I have suggested earlier, it is a very good idea to talk to an accountant or business specialist to help you chose the right structure for your startup.

If there are co-founders, then things get a little trickier!

Should I Incorporate with co-founders?

Why is it trickier? Let me present you the following question that I want you to think about. Who deserves the larger share of a business at the beginning, the guy with the money or the sales guy? What if the guy with the money only contributes money and nothing else? What do you think?

Now complicate matters more by introducing more co-founders, a marketing genius, and a great business builder. What do you think now?

Sweat equity vs. financial equity.

When a business morphs from startup to successful going concern, more is demanded of the co-founders; more time, more energy and more hard work. When someone has an equal share of the company and does nothing as it grows, it is incredibly demotivating for the other co-founders and, needless to say, destructive.

It's vital that before you commit time and money with co-founders, you need to have agreements in place, and unfortunately, you need to be prepared to enforce them legally. I know that seems hard assed but this is now a business, and it's just as much your investment as any of the other co-founders. Where an investor puts money in the startup and does not contribute anything more, then that person is the dispensable one in the team.

Therefore, it is a good idea to incorporate, BUT with a clear understanding of the commitments that each co-founder has with the business. If it is felt that one of the co-founders cannot, or will not be able to grow with the business, there must be an opt-out or first right of purchase with the other co-founders. Quite often this mechanism is built in at incorporation where the other co-founders agree on a buyout price in advance with the financier. For example, a co-founder agrees to put in $20,000 as seed capital. He or she then agrees to a buyout figure of $50,000 within two years or the shares convert into equity, i.e., he or she becomes a full voting member of the company.

With co-founders, you will have to work out the value of sweat equity to finance equity and get on with it!

Misunderstandings will destroy a business when the going either gets tough or when it's doing well, so it's better to sort these things out at the beginning.

Stage 2 - Liftoff

"Strive not to be a success, but rather to be of value." **Albert Einstein**

Chapter 7 - Strategy

Start with the end in mind.

When Stephen Covey wrote his famous book *7 Habits of highly effective people*, there was one habit that grabbed my attention, and it was *to start with the end in mind*. It's so simple to grasp. Just going back to the map analogy in a previous chapter, you wouldn't start out on a journey without having a destination - would you? Well, it's amazing how many people do, especially when starting out in business.

When it comes to formulating strategy, you need to go back to something we considered at the mindset stage - the *why* we are doing this? One of the businesses I set up with two others was founded on the basis that we would develop it until it reached the financial targets we had set, and then we would sell it. We started the business with the end of our involvement in mind; we started and developed it to sell. Period!

This end aim is important to consider because the strategies we adopted were done to achieve that goal! Now, when you align your corporate strategy with what you want to achieve personally from your business startup, it's incredible the power of focus you will find to fulfill that aim. That is why starting with mindset and planning are so important.

From the beginning - plan to make yourself redundant!

A truly successful company is one where the owners work *on* the company and not *in* it. I know you have probably heard this many times but what does it mean?

Many entrepreneurs and business owners start up a company for various reasons, and the most common two are firstly, the person can't imagine working for someone else, and secondly, the person wants more freedom, and not be stuck in the nine to five employee scenario.

Working in your business means you have created a new job for yourself! You are tied to working in your company for your salary. You have become your employer. Now that may seem that's what you wanted after all - complete independence, you are now paying your way, but is it? When you work in your business, you create a personal boundary that limits your potential and others around you to participate. It is you being a manager and not a leader.

When you create a business there is an enormous amount of work that you have to do yourself - I know I've been there! However the business will grow, it will grow in terms of sales and personnel. The way you manage that growth from the start will determine the level of success you have. The demands on your time differ in nature as the business expands. Your initial me and myself alone, or my co-founders and me, becomes progressively more people, and you find that you have to delegate and manage more as a first step, that is a natural progression in business.

Here lies the danger that you do not change that mode of operation. Many business owners get set into a routine. By managing, and I mean micro-managing, the entrepreneur believes that this is the crucial linchpin to the business. His or her business has become a part of the persona and this is where things often start to unravel.

When a business becomes founder dependent - then the business becomes the founder. Think about that statement, it's quite deep. What it means essentially is that if anything happens to the founder, then the business as an entity will have difficulty surviving.

In this situation, it is often difficult to retain trained and skilled staff, the lifeblood of many businesses. It's a fact; unfulfilled and unhappy staff leaves no matter what the pay benefits are. Highly skilled or experienced people always have value, if not to you, then to a competitor.

When your business expands, you keep doing management things. In this doing, you are using your time working in the business completing tasks that an employee could now be trained to do. Yes, there are certain functions you should retain, and we will talk about that later, but 95% of what you are doing can be given to others.

The best businesses are those where there is a clear leader that strategizes to create value leaving the management to manage. The best startups are those where the company starts with a manager who is also a leader; a person who sees the big picture, i.e., the end in mind and goes for it. Now, don't get me wrong a leader also has to manage but not micro-manage.

Create a company built on systems, not people.

You may be asking, how can I do this at the startup stage? You need to develop processes as you go along. When something works, document it. It must be repeatable. When something is documented and repeatable by others, it becomes a training manual. At this stage, your employee can take on the task, which is especially relevant in a product creation environment, whether it's software development or some types of manufacturing. It is especially the case in franchise companies.

You have to develop from the inception of the company

a systems friendly approach, and this does not detract in any way from the job satisfaction of your employees, if done right. In fact, employees feel more secure when there is a set of guidelines, and they feel managed and supported. Where the balancing act from the entrepreneur comes in, is allowing the employee the freedom to do the job they have been trained to do without being micro-managed. You see, when you manage processes and systems, the people don't feel the pressure of management, which is more liberating than suffocating.

As the company develops and expands, the employees and the managers should be trusted and encouraged to take on the role that you previously held. They should grow into the roles and feel supported. The purpose of managing this way, especially for management, is to build self-sufficient teams, and part of this process is to make the managers task independent, i.e., accept responsibility for making things happen that are necessary for the development of the company. As one of my previous clients said to me jokingly,

"I love it when I can go away for a holiday without my laptop and phone, with the only interruption allowed being someone to contact me if the house is burning down."

What you will see as the entrepreneur as the business develops, is you have got to the point where you can focus on taking time out from *doing* to *creating strategy and relationships* that grow the business going forward.

At this point, you work on the business instead of in it, and you can more easily exit the company without destroying what you have created.

Once you have the essential internal structure that promotes growth, internally you need to start looking at the support infrastructure that will enable you to continue working on your business.

Self-efficiency.

To bring about this, you need to apply an ordered discipline to your activities to achieve those things that are most important to you in developing the business.

Don't waste your time - it's the most valuable resource you have!

Everything that you do in your business should be focused on three things, increasing sales, increasing profits and brand development. If you're doing activities that are not aligned to any of these tasks, then you are wasting time.

You need to analyze what you do on a typical day, keep a diary and at the end of the day look honestly at those activities not focused on business development. Most times when you do this, it will shock you how you could use your time better.

I've been guilty of it myself! I used to allocate thirty minutes a day for catching up reading emails etc., and when I added that time up it came to ten hours a month of productive time that I could have spent doing other tasks, that's over a working day a month! Would you seriously spend a full day at work reading emails? I doubt it. When you break up activities like that, it starts to add up. Don't get me wrong reading your emails and keeping informed is vital, but you need to systematize it.

My solution was simple; I created an email address for my primary contacts and another for the not so important ones. These email addresses were never mixed, and this simple adjustment cut down my time reading emails to six minutes a day, once in the morning first thing and about 4 pm. You will find in business that these are the times when urgent things can get done!

Plan your day.

Once you are aware of how valuable you time is then, you plan your day. You see, it's pointless planning your day first if you don't have a yardstick by which to measure what's important, and those are the three things mentioned above. You have to make the most efficient use of time to achieve the day's tasks, and that is done by creating a daily plan. It doesn't have to be complicated - it just has to reflect those things that need to get done to achieve the development of the company.

For example, my last task before I finish for the day is to prepare a *to-do list,* I call it my TDL. I order what is the most pressing need to be done and then the next and so on. I do not include more than six tasks on any one day. As tasks get done, they get crossed out on the list. I do not immediately update the list. I wait until the end of the day. The next days' list is filled with the new priority tasks plus those that are outstanding to be fulfilled. This way I find that the priority tasks are always taken care of first. A few years ago I went over my diary and did some analysis and found that 95% of the top priority tasks were achieved; this is such a small sounding thing to do, but it has incredible focus power, and it's amazing what you get done with it.

Do what's most important first.

We alluded to this with the TDL mentioned beforehand. It's so important to re-iterate that all your tasks should be aligned with the three things that you, as the entrepreneur, must achieve. After you have done the TDL, look at it again and make sure that the number one priority there deserves to be there. You also need to be aware that there is a hierarchy of priorities, and this can be fluid. Sometimes the top priority is ongoing. For example, one of my clients involved in high-tech manufacturing had incredible problems with suppliers that provided finishing services. Deliveries were always late, and this caused bottlenecks in the company's production line, and was a primary cause of cash flow problems as they were not paid until the finished and assembled product was delivered to their customers.

This was an on-going problem and the priority task of the company to sort out. As you can imagine, it was not one of those problems that could be sorted in a day. As a solution, it was agreed with the main company responsible for the delays to lease a particular machine within their factory, and dedicate it to supplying my client. It took two months to get this solution! This problem remained priority number one for two months!

Adopt useful technology early.

Everything you use in the business, especially technology, must be necessary and useful. I have seen entrepreneurs needlessly spend money on the newest laptops, PCs, and phones before investing in other mission critical hardware and or software.

There are two uses of technology within your company,

personal use, and business use, and the two should not be confused. You should always put the purchase of technology necessary for running the business first. I have seen entrepreneurs spend $10,000 on the latest laptops and phones for themselves and their family before spending anything on their business, and later when the company needs more finance it isn't there! No wonder!

For personal use all you need these days are a phone with email capability, a laptop, and the internet access. You can buy or lease better models later when the business develops. The critical thing is, where technology, such as a PC or network system for staff is needed, this takes priority.

During the initial planning, you should have completed an audit on what technology is required to run the company efficiently. You should, however, have identified during the planning stage, what technology will propel the business forward faster; this is the technology that you should invest in and adopt early. If an investment now will increase your revenue substantially, then look at it as an investment and not a cost

The peril of putting your business before family.

When you are about to start your business, you have to have your stakeholders with you. Stakeholders are those who have a direct interest in the business, whether it is co-founders and or family members. Fail to keep your stakeholders happy and you're in trouble, maybe not immediately but certainly later down the line.

The reason you need to do this especially with family members is the utter focus and concentration that you have to devote to the business at startup stage. If your family members, in particular, your spouse, are not fully aware or onboard of the commitment, you may have to give up one or the other.

The amount of successful but divorced business people I have met is higher than the national average. There's a cost-benefit to everything, but remember this, if your business is successful and it costs your marriage - you could lose fifty percent of it through the divorce courts! So quite literally make sure your family bonds can take the strain.

Outsourcing and startups.

Many entrepreneurs work incredibly long hours with high-stress levels, which can have negative consequences as, mentioned above, but it doesn't always have to be that way. If you analyze the work you do while starting up, you would be surprised how much of it you don't have to do which costs you more by trying to do it. Under these circumstances, capital permitting, it's best to outsource certain tasks, especially administration.

Typical administrative tasks that can be outsourced are secretarial services. For example, there are many virtual office companies that supply a phone answering and mail service.

If the business is service related, meeting rooms and conference facilities can be rented from companies like Regus, which are located in many cities in various countries throughout Europe and the U.S.

It is also best to outsource accounting tasks; again many agencies offer competitive rates. Most people aren't accountants, and one thing you cannot afford to have is a problem with the Internal Revenue Service - it's not worth the hassle. You should, of course, keep track of invoices and cash flow, especially the bank balance. You should always know the cash flow position of the company, but the paperwork can be outsourced.

Another major benefit to the startup is temporary staff outsourcing. For example, where the startup is product-centered, temporary staff can be hired for the day and by the hour for assembly, delivery and a host of other tasks that can free you, the entrepreneur, to focus on generating more sales.

Are any customers or clients vampires?

I'm serious here! Some customers will suck the life-blood out of a business. For the amount of profit they generate compared to the amount of time expended on them, they are unprofitable. I know it's difficult to turn away customers at the startup phase of a business and technically speaking you shouldn't; think of it like this. When you hire a staff member, you would sensibly hire them on a probationary basis, which is usually three months. Why shouldn't you apply the same principle to your customers? From experience, it doesn't take long to find out which customers take most of your time for the least amount of profit generated.

From day one you should keep track of the invoices generated and time it takes for invoices to be paid if you are not being paid up front, i.e., credit (which isn't a good idea at the beginning of the startup). If you find that some of your clients are late payers or worse non-payers and a disproportionate amount of time is used to chase up the bills in comparison to the income they generate you have two options. Firstly, invoice for immediate payment, or secondly fire the customer. I know, it sounds counter-intuitive, but believe me; nothing takes more resources out of a startup than chasing late or non-payers.

Remember, cash flow is king, and you're not a bank

supplying credit to a customer! Time spent chasing up the laggards is time spent not developing your business and getting the right clients for your business.

This is one place where you need to apply the *Pareto Principle*, the 80/20 rule where 80 % off your profits come from 20% of your clients or customers. These are the guys you have to look after. These are the life-blood of your business!

It's OK to make mistakes!

Great strategy that propels your business forward doesn't come out of thin air. Your startup should be viewed as a machine. Things can and will go wrong, and when they do you should look on these as learning experiences and learn from them, and not create a blame culture, either blaming yourself, employees or worst of all your clients or customers! Mistakes should not be repeated, so that is why if it is linked to a process or some aspect of training, that it is documented so the fix becomes part of the culture of doing business in the company.

Making mistakes is part of the learning process of making yourself redundant and maximizing the input of your employees. Employees that are empowered will make mistakes, if you punish them for doing so, you will kill the business in the long term. Your people are one of the greatest assets of the company - don't abuse their trust in you as a leader!

As the entrepreneur, you should not let ego get in the way of recognizing when you have made a mistake, especially one that involves strategy. You should not beat yourself up about it, you just move on and learn from it, and do it quickly. To some extent, this harks back to the section on the growth mindset that we covered at the beginning of the book.

Take heed of the economic cycle.

What do you mean by this I hear you ask? The economic cycle is a bit like the familiar product life cycle that you hear about in marketing books, but instead of representing the position you have relative to your direct competitors, it's the position you find your enterprise in the general economy. For example, there are three cycles, the boom cycle (2003 to 2007), the bust cycle (the Crisis of 2008) and the recovery cycle (2011 to 2015). Needless to say, if you started your business in 2008 at the height of the Crisis, you would have found finance almost impossible to get, so your strategies would have been different in starting up. Starting and surviving in a bust cycle is often the best time to do so.

Ironically, if you have cash, this is when you can get

equipment and labor more cheaply than at the top of a boom cycle, and very importantly you have access to a much higher qualified and potentially experienced team, as jobs can be scarce on the ground. Certainly, there is less cash around from consumers, but on the other side of the equation, there is likely to be less competition, as not everyone prepares adequately to survive a downturn and or recession.

If you start in a recession and prosper, it is much more likely that you will prosper even more in the recovery and boom cycles. The companies that start in a boom cycle often go to the wall more quickly.

I've seen companies that have started during the recessions of 2000 and 2008/9 grow incredibly strong during the recovery cycle as the entrepreneurs had to start the business more frugally and with greater thought and imagination.

These disciplines are rarely lost! In my view, bad economic times represent a great opportunity with the right mindset!

Chapter 8 - Marketing and Sales Strategy

Marketing and Sales.

Is there a difference between marketing and sales?

Marketing and sales are two different functions in business. Many entrepreneurs do not understand the difference, and it is a crucial one to grasp. Also, that *the market* and *marketing* are two different concepts.

The market is a demand and supply mechanism where buyers and sellers exchange financial consideration for value, i.e., a price is agreed, and a transaction occurs. Marketing is nothing more than simply a process whereby you influence the actions of others to buy what you're selling. Any other definition is purely academic.

In a nutshell, good marketing is about understanding your customer, what makes him or her tick, what are the buying triggers, competitive positioning and importantly what are the *sellable benefits* of that product or service, and apply that knowledge to the market.

If your product has been market tested, i.e., that there is demand, and it is sellable at a profit, then the selling is made easier through marketing. If however there is no market (demand) for your product and or service, then you are not going to be able to sell that item. All the marketing in the world won't change that. One may be tempted to argue that Steve Jobs created a new market by creating the iPod - but did he? No, through clever marketing he created a niche within an already existing market, which was downloadable music on a very *cool* mp3 player. He built his business model around supplying a need that already existed; there was already a market!

Your customer is king!

You must focus on your customer. Without customers, you don't have a business. This is stating the obvious, but it's amazing how many entrepreneurs fall in love with the idea of their business product, thinking it's the most wonderful product or service in the world without thinking of their customer or end user, and then scratch their heads in disbelief when the product does not sell.

Back in the feasibility plan and proof of concept stage, I suggested that it is vital to create a customer avatar. You need to visualize your customer. Who is he or she? What hurt or need are you trying to address? What motivates your customer? What is the demographic profile of your customer?

It's when you get into the mind of the customer and

start seeing what it is that motivates them, is when you can start tailoring an effective customer and client acquisition program.

Smart marketers know that it is four times harder to get a new customer than it is to keep an existing one. You keep existing customers loyal by giving them more value than they perceived they have bought. For example, better after-sales service, a high-quality product. Your customers know when you go the extra mile! That is why, when the business's marketing is customer focused, it's so much easier to cross-sell and upsell products or services.

A perfect example of a major corporation losing focus on their customer in the 1990's was Kodak. As a corporation, they failed to see a major technological change in their market. Their marketing people failed to see the effect that the digital camera revolution was going to have on film. Fuji, their major competitor, did, and the result, just ask yourself the question - how many Kodak digital cameras do you see compared to Fuji? Not as many! They did not know their customer!

When you know your customer, their needs, their desires and what market they operate in, then you can create relevant and targeted marketing strategies, which is then reflected in the type of advertising you direct to the customer profile. For example, your research may show that radio advertising is much more effective than TV adverts because your target audience tends to commute by car, and are more likely to be listening to the radio than have the time to watch TV later in the evening.

Another example I will share with you was with a client that had a chain of Italian restaurants. He was looking at creating a better service, and at the same time increasing sales turnover during the quiet days of the week.

What we noticed during one evening at one of his restaurants when we were discussing some strategies was the number of patrons that had their mobile phones on the table while they were eating. Yes, I know it could be construed as bad manners in polite society, but it was an eye opener.

We decided to experiment with building an SMS (text) list. The decision was made to train the reception staff when they received a booking call to take the details and ask the patrons while on the phone if they would like to be included on a text list for information on new additions to the menu and special offers.

This exercise was extremely successful and over the course of six months, nearly five thousand numbers were added. Every two weeks one thousand texts were sent on a rotational basis so as not to overuse the list. These texts were aimed at filling seats on Tuesdays and Thursday evenings when the restaurants needed a boost. The turnover from this marketing tool increased by 17%. The feedback from the patrons was extremely positive; they felt that the owner was providing an excellent service, and they appreciated being informed when specials and new menu items were added.

This example is a good real world illustration that observing customer or client behavior can be an excellent way of providing a greater service, and adding value to the business. In this instance, the patrons felt that they were the center of attention. It was a win-win situation!

A confused mind says no!

Your message that you get out to your customers should be made as simple and understandable as possible. There should be no ambiguity about the benefits and solutions that your product or service addresses. If there is any confusion in the mind of your potential customer, you've lost them. As I said a confused mind says no!

This is a major reason why you have to get to know your customer intimately, in a way you have to become the customer. I can't stress this strongly enough.

Sell the benefits, not the features.

Research shows that customers buy products on impulse and emotion. They then spend time rationally persuading themselves that they have made the right decision. When you sell the benefits of a product or service, you are appealing to the emotional solution that the customer needs to satisfy. That, as I explained before, is the enabling of the purchase decision necessary for the sale. When you market the features of a product or service, you are appealing to the rational side of the persons' brain that will be more attuned to decide negatively. The purchase is not attractive to them.

An example to illustrate this fact is the smartphone market. Smartphones today all text, have the Internet and host a whole plethora of apps, so the use of the features of a phone is broadly the same. However, one particular brand stands out, the iPhone. Now, don't get me wrong here I'm not doing Apple any special favors, just illustrating a point. This phone is high quality, durable and expensive. Its benefits are sold, not its features. For example, Apple has iTunes, so you can listen to your favorite music anywhere. The phone has Facebook and a very strong anti-theft app, has an extremely user-friendly platform, very reliable and, very importantly, has *street cred*. For example, go to any Starbucks and see how many people are using iPhones and Macs. Apple sells benefits!

It's sales that matter!

Be under no illusion the purpose of marketing is to increase sales revenue and, therefore, directly add value to the business. Whether you like it or not, most of the strategies that you adopt should be focused to add value through the sales effort. Without sales the business is dead.

As an entrepreneur, your first task is to get sales. You even had to get sales in your proof of concept to verify your business model, and nothing has changed. Your sales force is equivalent to a fighting army moving forward with every other function in the business providing logistical support. More sales at a higher profit margin than your cost of capital is a victory over your competitors. You always have to be selling.

As the entrepreneur, you are in sales, not marketing. The marketing is providing intelligence support; it's sales that are delivering the punch. However, as soon as you can, you need to replace yourself with sales people that are better than you are. Your first task in the business is to fire yourself as the sales person and hire somebody better!

Every, and I mean every successful businessman, has had to be a successful sales person first. The idea had to be sold to investors, the products or services had to be sold to customers or clients, and there probably were times of doubt that you even had to sell the business to the rational side of your brain to keep you motivated during the hard times. So, to some extent sales are in your blood.

All the successful startup entrepreneurs I have ever met, could sell. Obviously some better than others, but I can't remember any that hadn't any sales experience during the startup.

As a startup matures to the going concern stage, the sales strategies change, this is common and desirable. Nothing teaches like experience. You will find what strategies are more effective to close that sale, which sales staff is best, and you will learn how to optimize the marketing to support the sales effort.

You should market yourself.

As the startup entrepreneur, you're the front man. You're the brains and the creator of the business. When building the business, you are marketing yourself as the person, i.e., the company to do business with. You have integrity, intelligence, a go-getter attitude, reliable, and importantly you provide what you promise.

Remember, at the startup stage, the only thing your clients or customers are buying into without a track record is You! So, to sell the products and or services your business provides you are in a way selling yourself when marketing the company.

This couldn't be truer when you are networking and when you are at your local chamber of commerce building up useful connections and potential clients.

You do not get a second chance to make a first impression!

It is of vital importance when selling that you never promise anything that there is a chance you can't deliver. If you are in doubt about a deadline, it is better to be honest, and upfront. This sounds counter intuitive but in my experience when I was upfront about a potential problem, I won more business than I lost but, more importantly, I was able to keep a good relationship with the customer.

It is in a way a gamble, but it does pay off in the end. If the person gives you their business, then you should aim to fulfill the order or project ahead of time and add extra value. This attitude creates an incredibly powerful first impression and is vital to establish trust in the client/customer relationship going forward.

It is also a fact of life that people don't like change - so if they're happy dealing with you, then you have established a commercial relationship that you can effectively build upon. Remember, you are always dealing with people, not things, and this will help you focus more on the customer and his or her needs first.

Copy what works.

Copy what works with your competitors, except do it better. If you think this is sleazy and unethical, think again. The Japanese in the 1970's built their car industry on copying European cars, especially the small economical ones, and made them more reliable and fuel efficient. As a car industry, they are still reaping the rewards; think about it, how many Toyotas and Hondas do you see?

When you copy what works and at the same time differentiate yourself by making some adjustments to improve their system, you are doing two things. Firstly, you are saving yourself time and money by not making the mistakes your competitors made in perfecting their system, and secondly, you are removing some of the risks when starting up.

If you decide to copy the successful elements, make sure that those elements are copyable. For example, it is much harder to replicate a sales system built on an existing network of contacts. What you should look to replicate and improve on, are their sales systems and strategies where possible.

Build a sales and referral network.

Don't be myopic when it comes to getting sales. Strategies that improve the sales figures and at the same time keep costs down are excellent strategies to pursue. Many startup entrepreneurs see sales as a component of their own efforts. Let me explain. Many entrepreneurs when establishing a business see sales as a result of their efforts or their direct staff. They feel and need more control over the process. Sometimes this is the result of insecurity borne out of a fear of failure and or a need to keep profits from leaking out of the existing structure.

A more far-sighted entrepreneur sees things differently. Creating a sales network of affiliated companies or individuals is an extremely efficient and cost-effective way of getting sales. If the network is created correctly and the Remuneration is generous, then the risk of client leakage (stealing) is reduced.

Many service-based startups are very effective at using this referral system. For example, if you are in the process of setting up a financial services company that specializes in selling overseas property then it makes perfect sense to team up with attorneys and accountants who have clients that could be interested in buying those properties. You could, for example, have contacts in China who refer clients to your company for U.S. purchases. In such cases, a referral fee would be set up.

This referral network can be just as effective for a manufacturing or construction business as well. This is where you could, for example, build a great network using your local chambers of commerce. Also, government agencies are excellent sources of business. You can bid on tenders with the intention of becoming a preferred supplier. When you get this preferred status, it can propel your chances of winning contracts over your competitors. The bottom line here is to think outside of the box. Your sales strategy, should at startup, be geared to getting as many promoters of your business services and products without having an infrastructural cost.

The beauty of a sales referral network is that it doesn't cost you anything until a sale is made, so it keeps your fixed costs lower!

When a sales structure works.

Sales are best generated by utilizing a structured approach; as I mentioned before it could be through an internal directly controlled sales team and or the usage of a referral network. The fact is there has to be some structure. When the entrepreneur is the only sales person in the business, it is very easy for that person to create the sales process and memorize it. It is crucial that if this is the case, the entrepreneur documents the processes and produces a sales training manual. I said before that the first task that an owner has is to fire himself as the sales person. When the time comes to hire a sales professional, he or she is going to need guidance, a set of rules and especially some training about the product or service being sold.

I know it's true that there are sales professionals that could sell an igloo to an Eskimo - but what happens if that person leaves the business? You have to start again.

It is certainly worth considering that the best sales persons should share in the equity of the company. A great sales person or team can really kickstart a startup.

For salespeople, you have to have a generous remuneration package, if you want the best. Furthermore, non-performing sales people should be quickly replaced.

Do not be afraid to experiment. If you do, though, experiment on customers and or clients that will have a minor impact on your cash flow if things go wrong. You must understand and accept that it's ok to make mistakes, but since you are putting the customer first, if you do make one, then have some mechanism to put it right!

Red Lines that can't be crossed.

Within the sales structure, you should have a definite system of red lines that are not crossed, and these should be clearly communicated to all people in the sales process with a clear disciplinary process. In this instance you are not micro-managing the business, you are protecting it from brand damage at best and legal suits at worst!

I had a client that nearly lost her business because her telesales person promised additional benefits to obtain appointments with the potential customer. When the sales person arrived the potential customer would bring up the promised benefit to be included to close the sale; this showed three things, my client did not have sufficient control over the sales process, inadequate monitoring, and poor training.

There was poor communication in the sales department. The salesperson shrugged it off as he was still getting the sale, and the telesales person was seen to be effective because appointments were being made, and with those appointments, came the sales.

Under some circumstances, this would be acceptable, but with the company running very tight margins, the return on capital was negative. In other words the company was losing money on these sales. Sales were being bought, and as I said before this is a sure fire way of eventually losing your business.

This is such a dangerous tactic to adopt because the customers became accustomed to having added benefits for each repeat sale, and once that occurs, you have two options, re-educate the customer that they have to pay more and probably lose them, or fire the customer! In my clients' case, she lost 20% of her customers.

Needless to say, both the telesales person and the sales person were fired and a list of do's and don'ts were created in the company with a clearer documented sales process in relation to procedures and ethics.

However, even though, the sales person and telesales persons were fired, this to me was a significant management failure. So create a set of red lines that should not be crossed especially concerning ethics and behavior from the beginning.

Chapter 9 - Finance Strategy

Are you still in the twilight zone?

Would be entrepreneurs are either in a position to start their business as their primary source of income now, or are still dependent to some extent for their main source of income from a regular job, and are looking at transitioning. I call the transition stage the *twilight zone* because many people in this category want to start a business but often chicken out before taking the final jump. There's nothing wrong with that - it takes guts, passion and dedication to start a successful business, and quite frankly not everyone has what it takes.

Now the reason I bring this up is that I mentioned before in the reality check chapter, you have an extra step to progress through from holding down a job to becoming a full-time entrepreneur. Except for that step, there is little difference in the approach to getting the business off the ground.

Having done the feasibility study and the proof of concept, whether currently employed or not, you rarely can start a business and hold down a full-time job, and pull it off successfully. My experience has shown that those who have prepared their finances before leaving their job have a greater motivation to make the enterprise work, and their chances of success increase.

Hit the street running!

With the feasibility study, proof of concept and business plan under your belt, your main responsibility now is to generate sales sufficient enough to finance the business and pay your bills.

It is a dangerous myth propagated by so many startup gurus that you should pay yourself last. Anyone that suggests this, you should run a mile in the other direction. The only circumstances that you should not pay yourself from your startup are if you have no bills, somebody else is paying them or if you're still in your day job. Period!

Assuming you did your reality check, you should now be aware of your personal financial resources, and where you don't have enough cash flow to substitute what you earned while employed; then pay yourself what you can, especially mortgage or rent, and food. So many startups fail because domestic bill paying was not factored into the financial plan.

You have to hit those sales revenues with two budgets to pay, the company running costs and your household bills. Think of it - you wouldn't work for an employer for nothing! If you don't pay yourself, it means you are working for your company for nothing. Don't think of this as an investment in your future, and that you will pay yourself later. If you can't budget for your personal costs now, when will you be able to?

When looking at a business to invest into I always, and nearly every venture capitalist does this, find out what the owner(s) are paying themselves in the cash flow analysis. If I didn't see this, then the alarm bells went off, and nine times out of ten I wouldn't invest. Then I would look at what was a reasonable expense. Some wannabe entrepreneurs front-load their remuneration to sky-high levels to show the world in general, that they are high fliers with their company. Remember, that your costs have to be reasonable, even reflect a desire to cut down on superfluous expenses until the startup is financially well-grounded.

A good rule to live by is cash flow is king. Generate sufficient sales at a high enough profit to finance your personal and corporate expenses plus extra on top and you have a foundation to work on!

Focus on the cash flow!

If there is one piece of critical advice that I give to startup entrepreneurs, it's to get the business to positive cash flow as quickly as possible. That is you're covering your business expenses, whether that's inventory costs and or staff costs, your salary, commercial premises rent and utilities with profit. Too many businesses equate sales revenue with profit - that's a big mistake. There is sales revenue with profit, and then there is sales revenue at a loss. It doesn't take long for sales losses to destroy owner capital.

Matching cash flow.

Many failed businesses fail to manage cash flow whether it's from profitable sales revenue or not. Matching cash flow to the duration of invoices to be paid is a skill you're going to have to learn and get on top of as quickly as possible. You need positive cash flow to ensure you have working capital, especially in the early part of the startup, as you will not have built up a reasonable cash buffer in your business account. So, the last thing you want is either an extremely large cash outlay or a series of them before you have sales revenue in to compensate.

You should get into the habit of checking your bank balance, at least, every second day, until you have that sufficient buffer established that you are happy with.

Do not give credit.

As a general rule if you can't get credit don't give

credit and even better don't give credit at all. This sounds counter intuitive as you are probably thinking that you are not going to get business from large companies if you don't give credit. Well, think about this; larger companies generally do not give new customers credit. However, they insist on getting a minimum thirty days credit and can often be late payers. If you accept their credit terms and have no credit facility you have a thirty to sixty-day funding gap, and your startup company becomes a short-term financing facility for a supplier, or even worse a competitor. Insist on stage payments or payment up front and explain why.

If your company is going to be dependent on providing credit to a supplier or client, then firstly do a credit check on the company or client. Make sure they are credit worthy and can pay you. Secondly, if your business model is dependent on giving credit without receiving a payment grace period (credit), then you can consider setting up a revolving line of credit with your bank if your relationship is in good standing. However be aware that you may have to put up personal guarantees to get this. Another option is to look into getting an invoice factoring company to do business through. Be prepared to pay anywhere from 1.5% upwards for this service, and potentially you may also have to provide a personal guarantee. It certainly may be well worth looking into to ensure that you maintain the working capital crucial to stay in business.

Checks or card payments?

As a general rule, you should ask for checks for large items, and for smaller value items or services, cash or debit card. In the U.S., checks for large amounts are preferred and often have no bank charges associated with them. Credit cards and debit cards can have up to a 3.5% surcharge, so this is something that you will need to be aware of.

In the U.K. and Europe in general; most banks will charge for check and card transactions, so this cost has to be taken into consideration when pricing your products and services.

Pre-payment is best.

Where possible you should negotiate that customers or clients prepay all or a substantial part of the product(s) or service your business will provide. If the customer will not pay the entire invoice, then try and get your costs covered as a minimum at the time of the placement of the order with the outstanding amount to be paid on delivery. Pre-payment is extremely important for both you and the client. It is of the utmost importance if you operate a pre-pay system that you deliver, on time, every time. Once you fail to deliver, your client or customer will opt for credit and or take their custom to another supplier!

Debt management.

Many startup companies are started with debt financing, either through a bank or personal loans or credit card debt. Debt is like any other expense except for one thing - credit rating. Just like yourself, your company has a credit rating. If it doesn't have a credit rating, then it is in the process of developing one. Your customers or clients may choose to do a credit search on your company. If there are any late or non-payments, on say for example a company credit card, you may find a customer refusing to take the risk of either doing business with you or pre-paying, worse still you may not be able to get an overdraft facility from your bank.

All debt payments should be factored into your cash flow management and paid fully and on time, especially at startup. You do not know when or if you will need to go to your local bank with your cap in hand to request more money or an overdraft facility - so why take the risk!

Banks - Don't bank with one only.

You've heard of the expression don't put all your eggs in one basket - so why do most business people put all their business and personal banking through one bank?

It's a good idea to separate personal banking from corporate banking for this reason. I had a very painful lesson when I had a business failure! The bank raided my personal account to pay for business expenses - that's why! When you use one bank for business and your personal banking, the bank can transfer money from one internal account to another.

Some companies run more than one account in the same bank. That's ok to do as it makes sense. One of these accounts is often designated for paying taxes. For example, it is not unusual for an enterprise to separate sales tax or VAT, depending on where your business is domiciled. Also, some enterprises run a dividend account where profits are placed for payment later to the owners. It's often much more tax efficient to pay dividends to the owners than a salary, so many entrepreneurs pay themselves this way. The thing is to make sure those dividend payments are wired to your other bank when your accountant clears you to do so.

Banks guard their depositor's accounts like a thief guards his loot. So if you have your personal and corporate assets separate, it adds an extra layer of security and peace of mind.

Another way of reducing bank risk is to borrow from different banks or financial intermediaries if you need credit for the company. Many financial intermediaries will make loans to companies, for example, organizing leasing cars or vans. Additionally, invoice-factoring services can be organized through a different financial intermediary. It's good to spread risk!

Taxes - when to pay.

Tax regimes and tax payment systems differ on a country by country basis. They say that some things in life are unavoidable, death and taxes, and as far as businesses go this is both true and sometimes complicated. Corporate tax on profits is payable annually in the U.S. and the U.K., so providing you have made a profit you will have a transfer to make. In the U.S., you have a sales tax that is even more complicated in that it can differ from State to State, so this has to accounted for. The payment schedules for this tax in most cases can be negotiated to be paid quarterly.

In the U.K. and most of Europe, there is also a sales tax called VAT (value added tax), this is paid quarterly. Do not miss a tax payment. If you do you could expect to have a detailed tax inspection and the taxation authorities will target your company for a long time, often years. The downside to an inspection is that quite often the tax inspectors will not only look at the business they will look into your personal taxation affairs. So bottom line never mess with the 'Taxman'!

Get an accountant.

For not only the reason stated above, getting a good accountant is necessary. I say necessary because this is one area where he or she will save you money and time. Accounts and tax preparation must be done, and moreover, an accountant will be able to identify those areas where you qualify for rebates and or savings. Also, their fees are tax deductible, so it's a false economy not to use one.

Do not run before you can walk.

It's not only bad business strategy but also bad financial management to overstretch the finances of the company at any time, let alone during the initial startup phase.

It is very easy to get caught up in the euphoria of a business idea that takes off. Hey, it's great news but not necessarily the time to break out the champagne. Many businesses at startup receive an initial boost.

Have you ever noticed when a new restaurant opens up on the street how busy it is for a while and then it gets less busy. I call it the new kid on the block syndrome, and it typifies the tendency that some individuals and companies like to try out a new supplier, and then return to their original supplier, later.

In fact, when the business starts to gain steam it's the

best time to adopt a two-pronged approach. Firstly, fine tune the marketing and sales efforts, (as discussed in the last chapter) and fine tune and make more efficient the finances of the company. The best time to make the finances efficient is when the company is healthy and growing not when *triage* is needed.

At the breakeven point.

You should always keep track of cash flow, bank balance and your level of profit on sales. By doing this, you get a quick feel when the business is at the breakeven level. That is the point where the costs, including your salary, are covered by revenue. It is no accident that cash flow analysis for a startup in the business plan defines where the breakeven point occurs. It's also what investors look for in the financials and is often used to judge the plan's adherence to realism.

So many times breakeven analysis errs on assumptions that are wildly exaggerated, and it's best to be more conservative when making these assumptions. Overambitious sales assumptions, for example, can lead to the entrepreneur putting less emphasis on sales and marketing strategies, and again underestimating the breakeven point can result in too much emphasis on generating sales revenue. That's another reason proof of concept is so important.

Breakeven is an important metric for two reasons. Firstly, it is of immense psychological value as the reality now registers in your subconscious that your idea is now a business. The idea has become a reality. Secondly, when this important milestone is reached, business owners often take the foot off the pedal; it's a good idea to do this but just not now!

It's also the time that many business owners feel comfortable enough to expand the premises, refit the offices and possibly take out the lease on that new Mercedes you promised yourself. After all, you only have to fine-tune your business now to make healthy profits.

This is the point where you have to resist those urges. You should ideally utilize existing resources to breaking point. The greater boost you can give to the capital of your business now, the stronger it will be going forward. Remember, you're not foregoing rewarding yourself, just don't do it now!

At this point, you should look to see what further efficiencies you can integrate into the business. You can do this now because you know you are making sales and there is a track record of success, as well as failure. You should build upon your success to make the business better for your customers and clients.

It is at this stage you should anticipate demand stretch and pre-negotiate premises or facilities on a needs basis. You do not have to sign leases until you need to. The key is, to be prepared for expansion when certain financial and sales targets have been met. Remember, empty and redundant space costs money and reduces the amount of working capital for expansion. However, if your targets as mentioned earlier have been met, you need to be careful that lack of capacity doesn't impede healthy business growth.

For a service related business, most bottlenecks in acquiring new business relate to getting suitably experienced and qualified staff. You should hire new people when the current staff is nearly fully stretched, and the client acquisition process is in full swing. It is very easy for staff, in a service-based business to become overwhelmed, especially in I.T. and roles where personal client relationships are important. So special attention needs to be applied here.

Never, ever, buy business!

When a company starts up and begins to expand there is the temptation to expand sales revenue at any cost. Now, as touched on before sales revenue can be profitable or unprofitable. Where sales revenue is unprofitable, you are effectively consuming capital, your capital. There are many reasons why businesses fall into the trap of buying business, and one of them is to match sales revenue, i.e., income with expenses, in other words matching cash flow. Intrinsically there is nothing wrong with matching cash flow, and it must be done, but it's how you do it, that's incredibly important.

Profit, from sales, provides a working capital buffer. Losses from sales eat into working capital. Needless to say, working capital represents a snapshot of the liquidity position of the business at any one time. So, no working capital equals no liquidity, and no liquidity puts the business continuity at risk. Continuous losses in a company mean it goes out of business. Period!

So how does a business buy revenue? There are several ways, which include the product, or service not being correctly priced, in other words, costs have not been properly allocated and then a sufficient margin added; a sales person keen to meet bonus targets discounts the price too aggressively to get a sale. The point is that every product and service must be adequately costed and then priced for profit. To prevent this slow hemorrhage, this should be done with reference to *value creation*. Every aspect of the business should contribute to value creation in the business.

What is value creation?

From the outset, your primary financial strategy should be the generation of profits from a capital management perspective, geared towards value creation.

Put simply, value creation is managing the business to earn a return on the capital that is greater than the capital originally invested; this effectively means as the entrepreneur, you have to analyze how much capital you have, how your capital is employed and how you create value out of it.

So to start you need to calculate accurately the capital you have in the business; this will have been partially done when you did the reality check. To start with you add in the financial resources committed, the vehicles, plant and premises or offices, and then it's necessary to go a step further to accurately quantify the capital employed.

Under normal accounting rules, research and development (R&D), training and marketing activities are put down as expenses. I have always said to my clients that you have to add these back to capital employed to get a more accurate value of the capital you have used.

A good illustration of the importance of marketing and R&D as capital contributors is to look at companies such as Coca-Cola and GE. The brand value of Coca-Cola is immense; this required investment to build and still requires investment to retain it. The ingredients that go into Coke are more than likely similar to other competing brands, but the brand strength that Coke commands allows the company to charge a premium price and still maintain strong demand. The brand, and therefore by logic, the profit and value have been enhanced; this is value creation. With GE, its R&D is crucial to not only its' survival but also its profits. So, as an entrepreneur ask yourself this question; are the activities of Marketing and R&D enhancing the capital base or eroding it?

The short answer is enhancing it. So, marketing and R&D should be looked on as investments from your perspective. However, we are not finished yet; there is still one component that is often overlooked by many businesses.

At the startup stage your net operating profit figure will be low - so you are probably asking how can I get an accurate return on capital ratio?

When compiling the total capital value, you have to also consider equity. This becomes vital when you have an investor or investors in your company, which could be a bank or even friends or family. You have to calculate this cost of capital because your investors are expecting a greater rate of return for the risk being taken. For example, your rate of return from the business should be greater than an alternative investment choice available to the investor. An example will be if the investor has the choice of investing in a corporate bond that pays a coupon of 6% and you are offering 5% for equity, you are unlikely to get that investment. You are more likely going to have to pay more to reflect the extra risk to the investor, i.e., 8%.

Until you get cash flow positive and grow the net operating profit, you still have to use some datum. A good yardstick is to use a rate of return on equity that you would have paid for an investor in the business. Usually, an investor will require a higher return because of the risk involved, so there is a safe buffer in the percentage.

Added value is then achieved by managing the business to earn a return on the capital that is greater than the cost of that equity capital. This is referred to as economic profit or economic value added, and it is a very important metric, so it's better to use this strategy from the beginning.

As the business grows then, this ratio can be recalculated. The important thing here is to work out what your rate of return on capital is to create value and build from there. This is a strategy that will build your business solidly.

Chapter 10 - Your Business is About People

People are not economic units of production!

The primitive days when corporations thought of people as units of production are largely forgotten. If you ever start to see your staff as nothing more than a means to create your wealth, your company will never truly excel in providing the products or services that you want to sell.

Do not make clones of yourself by surrounding yourself with yes men and women. Where there is a sycophantic business culture, the business dies a slow death. To survive and expand a company needs different views on how to solve problems and take advantage of opportunities that arise.

Start small think big.

Your business mostly starts with one person, You! From the initial idea to fleshing out the reality it's your dream, but to make it a success you need people.

As a start, you need to carry people along with your vision to either invest in your enterprise or work for you. If you have co-founders, then you need people to work with you. One major skill you're going to have to develop is people skills, which in human resources jargon is referred to as soft skills.

To be honest, I would call many successful entrepreneurs that I have known as highly focused *benevolent manipulators*. Now, I don't mean this in a negative way, but there are times when as the entrepreneur you will have to overcome resistance, and the best way to do so is with persuasion, not force, or using your authority status as the owner. Remember, a bully gets things done out of fear (a short term gain), but a leader gets things done through inspiration, a long-term motivator.

A boss is all about power and control, and a leader is about inspiration and team building. If one of your goals is to sell your business as a going concern, then being a leader will help you make yourself redundant in a more commercial sense.

As your startup grows the number of people, you will employ will grow. Being a leader often involves simple things like knowing the names of your staff and a bit about them, making them feel appreciated and importantly, communicating to them the corporate goals, and how they help achieve objectives. Your employees need direction, but they also need praise when it's due.

However, there is also a delicate balance to be struck.

There must always be a divide. An unspoken recognition that while you are friendly, it's you who make the decisions. I have seen entrepreneurs get too close to their staff, with the result that it was difficult to replace the staff member that was not performing. The general rule is you should be friendly but not friends with your employees.

As the enterprise grows, staff that shows promise should be promoted, but only in so far as their capabilities are stretched. A stretched employee is easier to keep on board than an over-stretched (i.e., over-stressed) one.

Look for talent.

The nature of a business changes as it morphs from idea to startup, to going concern. Each of these stages requires different skill sets from employees, and the most valuable ones are flexibility and adaptability. More often than not, you are going to have to employ individuals who are more talented than either yourself or existing staff members. For example, I said earlier that the first role you should replace is yourself as the sales person. I'll be the first to admit while I get a buzz out of sales; I'm an amateur compared to many people out there. So, bottom line, talent rules. If you create a talented team around you, then solutions to problems and taking advantage of opportunities become so much easier and more profitable.

Money and what else?

It's not all about pay, but it helps. The fact is that talent costs. Every entrepreneur has to make talented staff feel motivated to stay. You see, talented people are always in demand. They get headhunted; they get offers that are difficult to refuse in relation to pay and benefits. So you have to find ways to retain your talent without breaking the bank - so to speak.

Some progressive entrepreneurs, before they hire somebody, find out about the person's attitude to work and home life. Many times, skilled and talented staff is after a balanced home life. For example, if they have a young family and have pre-school expenses, a benefit could be a special deal with a good pre-school or even having pre-school fully paid. For the family oriented staff, a benefit could be flexible working hours and or even some tasks that could be done at the person's home; this is more applicable for service based tasks.

Quite often, talented staff need role stretching and need to know that there is a support network.

The real challenge for the entrepreneur is persuading the employee to take the risk in joining the business. Remember, a high percentage of startups fail, and potential employees know this. It doesn't look good on an employees' resume if he has been employed in several short-term positions because the startups went broke. People want continuity and job security as they also have bills to pay!

Management by expectation.

There are plenty of management books out there and, believe me; I've read a lot of them. Some good, and many not so good, written by academics that haven't worked a day in the real world!

Believe me, people work so much better when they work towards something that they can internalize - an idea, an achievable goal something that they can personalize. You destroy this innate resource by micro-managing. I'm not saying that there aren't occasions to micro-manage, but they should be few and far between.

As the entrepreneur, you need to manage using three criteria. Firstly you need to make very clear what it is you want to be done. What the goal is. You discuss what's expected, how it will get done and how the success will be measured. You need to keep things clear and straightforward and assume nothing. Secondly, now that you have set the task/goal parameters you need to keep open frequent lines of communication. These criteria help to identify problems early and build trust between yourself and the group. Finally, reviewing that the goal and task have been realistically set.

If you find that the team is getting demotivated, confused and or resistant, then you have to be open-minded to reconsider and potentially adjust the expectation(s). You should not be scared of adjustment in light of the goals set and remember communication is the key element.

Don't let flexibility be seen as weakness.

Flexibility isn't about changing on a whim or adopting something that is not properly thought through. Flexibility is about being able and willing to change decisions, strategies and or the goals if needs be, in your enterprise.

The adoption of a culture of flexibility can encompass most of the elements of strategy, tactics and processes; that run congruently in a company. In fact, an inability to be flexible can hurt the company's bottom line. However, there is one element of flexibility that I would caution against, and it is changing the very *core principles* upon which the business has been started, as this will have the effect of destabilizing the whole business. In such a circumstance, being overly flexible to the point of changing the core values will cause strategic drift at best, and business failure at worst.

That is why it is so important to get the mindset right, the reasons for starting the business identified, and then pushing forward. It is crucial for your staff to know what the core values are, what the return on capital is, and where you see the company being in the future, i.e., providing the vision. You need to instill within the staff that it is ok to change elements of the business mix, as long as it is in reference to the core parameters.

Where changes and flexibility are aligned to these three criteria, change and, therefore, flexibility are seen as positives, and strengths and not weaknesses. Too often flexibility without explanation can be interpreted as weakness, and if that's the case, it will cause staff insecurity levels to rise. That is not desirable since this is is still a startup so not all the staff members are going to 100% trust their job security within their position.

When a clone is desirable.

One of the earliest pieces of advice I have mentioned is that you have to look at making yourself redundant. I have gone over some advice on how to do that, but if you're going to take more of a strategic role in the company, how are you going to achieve that?

Often the safest route is to *clone* yourself, but it isn't always the best solution. You need to find somebody who shares your same vision and strategic values. Now, having said that, you must realize that your clone has a different personality, and often has his or her way of doing things. Part of your leadership skills will be tested to the extent that you have to trust to a greater extent, your clones' abilities.

Many successful companies have a right-hand man, the heir apparent. That is the situation that you will have to foster in your business. Your people skills will, of course, be tested, your ability to trust will be tested, but to move forward at times, you have to let go. However, if you don't delegate this function you can't devote eighty percent of your time to business building. Remember the Pareto Principle we talked about in an earlier chapter! Remember if you're the *key* man, you most likely have a very complicated job but not a business!

It's the team that wins.

It's no coincidence that every team has a captain or a leader. It's the team that wins the Super Bowl or the NBA championship. Have you ever heard of the *star* player winning the championship for the team? No. The winners are the best teams from the top down.

The people in your company are a team, in fact sometimes many teams. Think of team and league management rolled into one! It's no coincidence that successful business people have often come from sports backgrounds!

When the Roman Emperors used to have a triumphal parade after winning a battle they had a slave whisper in their ear while on the chariot,

"Remember thou are not a god."

In other words, don't have a huge ego - when success comes, there have been other players!

This is why leadership is such a vital ingredient and deserves some examination in the next chapter.

Chapter 11 - Leadership

Share your vision.

Warren Bennis, a famous pioneer of leadership studies, defined leadership as,

"The capacity to translate vision into reality."

It's very simple; I like simplicity it's more readily understandable!

Vision in the context of your startup is what you want to do with your business, what you want to create and to get there. It has nothing to do with how you are going to get there - it's in the act! Leadership is action!

Your vision has to be translated into reality. To do this, you must lead. By de-facto you have, when you started your business, become a leader in name, but be careful there is a world of differences between a boss and a leader.

A great quote from Andrew Carnegie,

"No man will make a great leader who wants to do it all himself, or to get all the credit for doing it."

This quote so aptly defines this difference between boss and leader.

It's pretty clear, especially from what I have mentioned before, a boss micro-manages, a leader strategizes, and energizes others to make his or her vision into reality.

One of the critical leadership tasks is to share your vision, to have it adopted by others willingly, and make that vision simple and understandable by others. You can do this by leading by example.

Lead by example.

Some of the greatest leaders who have been great generals were often in front of their men. Julius Caesar fought alongside his Roman soldiers in the thick of battle, and could be seen inspiring his soldiers along the front line on his horse, when his major battle against the Gauls in France was almost lost. He inspired by sharing the burden of his men, sharing the danger and being seen! His example motivated his men sufficiently to risk life and death for him - it was not just for Caesars Glory, but the Glory of Rome!

Look at General MacArthur, when he stepped off the beach in the Philippines during World War 2 and said,

"I have returned."

His return was prophetic of the eventual victory! So simple, so inspiring and no wonder he is regarded by many people as one of the great leaders and generals of the war.

When a leader demonstrates how he or she will bring about the reality of their vision, respect is earned.

Earn respect.

A real leader earns respect; his or her authority comes from charisma, dedication and the ability to inspire, not just the capacity to command. Leadership based on authority alone, is not leadership - it's akin to a dictatorship, and we all know what happens to dictators eventually, their regimes fail!

Leaders gain respect by taking risks in the face of uncertainty and or danger. Leaders understand the saying - no risk, no gain.

Leaders take risks!

I'm not talking about the ultimate risk that has been starting the business; I'm referring to taking risks where the entrepreneur and or his team do not know the consequences of a decision, as there has been either no track record or experience gained from making that decision. It takes courage to take risks without knowing the outcome and whether the decision works or not - the courage is noted by the people of the company. However, there is a fine line between gamblers and risk takers, and it is often down to perception.

When a decision has been taken that goes well, most people think positively about the decision and call the entrepreneur a risk taker, but when it goes wrong, the entrepreneur is compared to a gambler. The perception that we humans have is that risk taking equals success, and failure equals gambling.

However, as a species, humans have only progressed on the back of risk taking, and that is why successful outcomes from taking risks are more attributable to leaders. This situation brings to mind the famous saying that,

"Victory has many fathers and defeat is an orphan."

Real leaders, therefore, are prepared to take on risk and prepared to fail, even lose it all!

To gain, you have to sacrifice.

Nothing in this world is free. You get something by paying for it or sweating for it! As a leader, you should inspire not perspire. I don't mean this in a sense of being lazy. Great leaders often work harder than most people appreciate. For example, Margaret Thatcher slept a maximum of four hours per night, and often Winston Churchill never slept at all. Their energy levels were incredible, because leaders are typically driven people. However, it is this myopic vision that can create and destroy at the same time.

Unfortunately, success can come at a price you would rather have not paid, and this could be regarding health, friendships and family relationships lost or badly impaired. However, most entrepreneurs are great at balancing aspects of their life because leadership is also about bringing people along with you on your journey! You just have to make sure that the price to get where you want to be is worth paying!

Work smarter and harder!

It's not just how hard you work; it's also how smart you work. It's about pushing yourself as much as you can, physically and mentally. As an entrepreneur, a startup will test your stamina to the limit. That is why you need to delegate as much as possible. If someone else can do the task better than you can, and more cheaply, the smart thing is to get that person to do it.

Much of what you do that separates leaders from managers is to push beyond your fears - your fear of failure in particular. I have come across entrepreneurs who have been successful only after several failures, and while these entrepreneurs learned from their mistakes, the one thing in common they shared, was they learned and tried again.

Any one of them could have given up, but what was more important in the end, was realizing their dreams. Being able to make their vision real was more important than the fear of failure.

Frank Herbert in his book *Dune*, had a simple statement that comes to mind here,

"Fear is the mind killer."

And it certainly is for many, but not quitters!

Working smart allows you to work hard on those things that matter in building your business. A good leader knows this.

Leaders are made.

Leadership is innate in most of us. It is circumstances and challenges met that demonstrate the ability of that leader. As in all things in life, talent will always outshine skill. Some people have a natural talent for leadership and never get the opportunity to display it, while others are highly skilled in the art of leading, and encounter the circumstances to demonstrate those skills. History rarely provides us with exceptionally talented leaders like Napoleon Bonaparte or Winston Churchill, so, for the most part; our leadership role models have leadership skills and some talent.

No one should ever doubt that they have leadership skills. If you're a parent, your children look up to you as leaders. If you're the choirmaster of your local parish choir, then you are a leader.

Therefore, when starting a business, you are now assuming the role of a leader, because whether you know it or not, that is what you are or are becoming!

Stage 3 - Consolidation

"The ones who are crazy enough to think they can change the World, are the ones who do."
Steve Jobs

Chapter 12 - Your Business is Changing!

When does a startup cease to be a startup?

There are two answers to this question. The first is when it fails and the second is when it morphs into a going concern.

Now, I call it a going concern because the company is on its way to maturity with systems in place that have propelled it out of the liftoff stage. The danger is, and pardon the pun, that it goes into orbit and stays there, without gaining escape velocity.

There is, therefore, another step of transition that goes from going concern to successful company. You may argue that any company that survives the startup and going concern stage is a successful company. No, not quite, in my experience, a going concern epitomizes a business that is surviving and not thriving. Businesses that are highly profitable or highly problematic are still going concerns, but a successful business is thriving, growing and highly profitable!

The relief that many entrepreneurs feel when the business can stand on its own two feet is palpable, and this is understandable, but the work is still a work in progress.

Do not ease off the pedal!

There comes a point in time that it is evident to those concerned in the startup, that things have progressed in the business and that things are different. Many entrepreneurs do not realize that this is the finish of the *getting the business of the ground* phase. Many business owners in failing to understand this see no reason to revisit their strategies to see if they are still compatible with the new paradigm.

This ignorance represents a lost opportunity, and it makes the difference between a successful company and one that is merely surviving. That is why it is so important to keep driving the business forward, and at the same time doing more fine-tuning on some aspects of the business, and change other aspects entirely.

Change management.

At the post-startup stage, you will be aware that certain foundational strategies are still strong, and you will know these work. However, you will see that growing has its' problems. Your business has grown from a child to an adolescent so the way you manage your relationship with it, must also change.

You have to manage change in a positive way. However, to manage change you have to be aware of what is changing. The changes are often quite noticeable but ignored. When change is ignored and not harnessed something often happens in the business - a crisis!

You see, people don't like change, most entrepreneurs do, but not everyone else in the business does. Change can be frightening, threatening and unpredictable. When a business expands after startup, what were relatively straightforward but challenging roles, become more complex and less challenging, because a set of rules, call them strategies and tactics, have been developed and are now operable, so a *system* is in place.

The accounts clerk that you hired when there were thirty customers now has to deal with two hundred. She now has to deal more frequently with late payers or non-payers and finds she needs an assistant who she has to train. She hasn't done that before. So now she is doing her job at a higher level, and training, as well. Soon the number of clients grows to five hundred. At this level, the old systems start to creak, and a new I.T. system is installed. Are you beginning to get the picture? Growth entails more complexity and greater demands from existing staff, with greater adaptive skills needed. That is why many people who participate in a startup business, which flourish, flounder when the business is up and running.

As I have mentioned before, you need to systematize roles, operations, and processes as much as possible because, believe me, if you don't put change management capabilities in early, there will be a crisis later that will force you to do so.

For example, one company that I dealt with, a trading company, sourced many of its products from China using Alibaba and sold those products online. When the business was starting, the goods came in via pallets and were shipped by sea. The pallets were stored in a secured warehouse. Over the course of nine months, these pallets became containers. The owners of the business had not fully thought through their inventory storage requirements for a growing business and managed inventory on an ad-hoc basis.

Unbeknown to the company they were not aware that the warehouse had been used as a guarantee by its owners for a business loan that went bad, and the warehouse owners filed for bankruptcy. As a result, the court froze their assets, including the warehouse and its contents. Without going into further details, this blew a substantial hole in my clients business and nearly destroyed it.

As the company grew, the entrepreneurs (two co-founders) had focused on building the online platform and the product sourcing, but had not amended their inventory strategies. Their company was growing; they focused on growth and ignored the obvious change that growth meant higher inventory requirements, i.e., space, access, and security. Needless to say, the solution the clients opted for was to bring inventory management under their direct control. If this change had been planned for, this crisis would have been avoided!

Investment for growth.

The transition stage just after startup is when expansion pressures become evident. The business has a new dynamic and an upward trajectory. The entrepreneur at this point often has the difficult choice of growing organically, i.e., more slowly, by utilizing working capital resources and avoiding debt, or taking on debt and using that debt to grow. However to grow, that debt must be invested to return a profit that is greater than the cost of capital, and so should be ideally invested in working capital.

The thing is, at this stage many businesses take on debt to pay for new cars and other non-essential investments. Quite often the owners take out money as drawings or as dividends to fund lifestyle choices, and this is a danger period, for debt improperly used, will reduce working capital and impede growth.

I'm not saying debt is a bad thing or should be avoided. On the contrary, debt is good where it is used to fund expansion and is costed as part of the capital, and the addition of debt results in a recalculation of the capital ratio, so as every investment and process reflect that increased cost of capital. Growth, with or without debt must provide an economic profit.

It is at this juncture that the entrepreneur must make a difficult decision.

The big decision!

Stay or sell? Most entrepreneurs that I have helped have wanted to start a business, grow it and run it. Few, however, have understood that the skill-set needed to start a business and then run it successfully, are different.

This lack of understanding is one of the reasons why you see so many successful startups with great promise, flounder soon afterward and it's a great pity to watch, knowing how much energy goes into starting a business.

There are a special few who manage to make the transition from startup to a successful business. They have adapted and succeeded.

I have, while in the venture capital field, worked with

serial entrepreneurs. To me, these guys and girls are a special breed. They build businesses to sell them - that's their business, and the one's I have had the pleasure of doing business with, have all been exceptionally successful at doing what they do. Many of them didn't start out that way. In fact, the successful ones had failures after the business was started. As I said before, we learn from failures, and these guys did!

Their business plan was simple. Build a real business from scratch. Systematize the processes and make themselves redundant, so as they could sell. They often put together an excellent management team and then came to us to find a buyer. More often than not, these businesses were sold to the management as a management buyout. Everyone was happy. The motto for many of these startup specialists was - *Next*!

The last word.

I have taken you through the main lessons that I have learned through working in venture capital, starting my businesses and working as a consultant. One of the secrets to a happy and prosperous life is to learn from the experience of others who have already made the mistakes that make life interesting, to say the least.

If I have to leave you with two pieces of advice, the

first is never give up on your dreams, ideas eventually become a reality if you persevere through good times and bad times, and secondly, get out there and do it and give it the best you can.

You will never know what you are truly capable of if you don't try!

Thank you for reading my book..

I would like to say thank you for taking the time to read, Startup: Be the successful entrepreneur you want to be.

If you feel that it has been helpful to you, please consider telling your friends or posting an honest review. Word of mouth is an author's best friend and much appreciated.

Good Luck….

Frank Burke

www.ingramcontent.com/pod-product-compliance
Lightning Source LLC
Chambersburg PA
CBHW071446180526
45170CB00001B/488